How to Cook a Coyote

Also by Betty Fussell

Mabel

Masters of American Cookery

Eating In

I Hear America Cooking

Food in Good Season

Home Plates

The Story of Corn

Crazy for Corn

Home Bistro

My Kitchen Wars

Raising Steaks

Eat, Live, Love, Die

How to Cook a Coyote

a Coyote

The Joy of Old Age

Betty Fussell

COUNTERPOINT * CALIFORNIA

HOW TO COOK A COYOTE

This is a work of nonfiction. However, some names and identifying details of individuals have been changed to protect their privacy, correspondence has been shortened for clarity, and dialogue has been reconstructed from memory.

First Counterpoint edition: 2025

ISBN: 978-1-64009-738-4

The Library of Congress Cataloging-in-Publication data is available.

Jacket design by Nicole Caputo
Jacket image of author © Macduff Everton
Book design by Laura Berry

COUNTERPOINT
Los Angeles and San Francisco, CA
www.counterpointpress.com

Printed in the United States of America

1 3 5 7 9 10 8 6 4 2

For Tucky and Sam and Paul

That is the only justification for my writing, living.
How one enjoys food now: I make up imaginary meals.

VIRGINIA WOOLF

*

Feast on your life.

DEREK WALCOTT

Contents

How to Cook a Coyote

A KNOCK AT THE DOOR

Tick tock.

Knock knock.

Who's there? Come in, come in. Step into the light. I'm all but totally blind, you know, and you're just a smudge among shadows. Come closer so I can see you. Closer.

Ah. Is that you, dear reader? Thank God you're here. For a moment I thought you were someone else. My dinner guest comes early, though he's never early, is he? Never late either. Which is how I know he's coming tonight, as soon as the last light winks away.

Which means we don't have much time. When you're near blind like I am, it's always twilight, but I can tell by the coolness of the air outside that the real night's creeping closer. Sit down, sit down, don't mind the boxes half packed with my life's belongings. I'm moving from one room in the old folks' home to another, smaller room, one with more nurses' aides and fewer freedoms. In lieu of a kitchen, a microwave. No fire hazards allowed near the blind and senile. So it's good you're here now. You must be hungry. Smell that? Dinner's in the oven. I'll give you a nibble when it's ready. Don't leave without the recipe.

But you're hungry for more than food, aren't you? You're here because you're craving stories. All of my meat and gristle and bone gnawed off by almost a century in this body on this earth. You and my dinner guest, both hungry to devour my life.

You'll remember better than I do that my last memoir, *My Kitchen Wars*, was a belated coming-of-age story spanning my life from my birth in 1927 to the end of my marriage in 1980. That was a different kind of meal from what I'm serving now. This time, it's a coming-of-death story, a mystery where the conclusion is foregone. This time, it's not about nourishment—it's about hunger. Hunger hard as desire. An insatiable hunger for *more*—more food, more friends, more love, more life. Most important, more time.

And there's no one better to incarnate the mystery and the hunger than my Double, my Shadow Self, and my Dinner Guest: Old Man Coyote. Trickster creator of life *and* death in animus-god myths from our earliest human ancestors. Millions of years of lean survival, of hunger stalking the border of the night. He's out there right now, watching and waiting. Biding his time and biding mine too. Scavenger, predator, player. Coyote knows the story, and it's not just about eating—it's about being eaten. Being hunted, stalked, chased, and inevitably devoured by life itself.

I'm almost a century old, but my Shadow is millions of centuries older. And although now he is everywhere on the planet but maybe the poles, he was born and grew up like me in the West. In Middle America, at the waistline of the Western Hemisphere, bulging out above and below until he finally gobbled up the globe.

That's why a coyote skin, head to tail, embraces one of my living room chairs. His skull looms on one of my walls. His photograph for target practice is pinned to one of my rafters. These memento mori remind me of where I'm going. The only questions are *How?* and *When?*

Now, a wolf is another beast entirely. He's a macho man, a romantic villain. A black-leathered biker who rips off helmet and goggles to attack his prey. Did you know that a while back the common phrase *to keep the wolf from the door* meant not just "to ward off poverty or hunger" but also "to delay premature ejaculation"?

A wolf is sexy, as M. F. K. Fisher showed us decades ago when she wrote *How to Cook a Wolf*. A wolf is the kind of fellow she knew how to seduce by inviting him in to share her table, and how to defang by her skill of turning sludge into festal pudding.

By contrast, a wolf's cousin, the wolf-dog (prairie wolf?), is a slapstick comedian. He's always in disguise. Where a wolf would snarl and leap, a coyote would giggle and let go a fart. Where in America we nearly exterminated wolves, coyotes survived by playing the fool, immortalized by the inexterminable braggart clown created by Looney Tunes—Wile E. . . . . You know his surname as well as Road Runner does.

If you were starving in the wild, you could probably imagine gnawing a hunk of roasted wolf meat on a turnspit over a campfire if you'd managed to kill one. But a coyote?

That's why I'm cooking Coyote Pie. You've heard of Tamale Pie, no? A Depression-variant staple of cornmeal mush made into a tamale dough enclosing a layer of braised meat. Tonight, the braised meat is coyote. Mine won't be the only life we feast upon tonight. Flesh in the filling, blood in the sauce, a Holy Communion of duplicity, a feast of the wild within and without. Old friends, come together at long last to watch a last full-belly moonrise together.

Ask a seasoned hunter and he'll laugh in your face. "How wouldja find enough flesh to cook on a scavenger that's gobbled up everything from witchetty grubs to rotting carrion? Might as well eat a buzzard."

*

If you're wondering why anyone would *want* to cook a coyote, stick around.

Tick tock.

But wait. I'm getting ahead of myself. There's still time, just a little, and you're here now, dear reader. Have a drink, settle in. I'll tell you how we got here. And if I slip off midway through, no matter—you already know the ending.

TIMEQUAKE

The year 2012 was when all my shit hit the fan at once, leaving naught but a turd behind. By November, Hurricane Sandy had blown me from my blacked-out apartment in a New York stripped of power back to the West Coast, where I began.

Come to think of it, 2012 was my eighty-fifth year on Earth and the most tumultuous of my life. Privately and professionally. Professionally, my calendar was jammed with lectures, writing workshops, book interviews, and conference panels around the country. Privately, I was trying to get the hell away from the East Coast, where I'd spent the last sixty-five years.

I was trying to be orderly about it. I'd flown to California a full year before Sandy hit. At eighty-four, I knew it was time to pick the place for my

Final Move. I wanted the sunshine, birds, bees, and trees of my original homeplace, but not the inland desert. I wanted to be lulled to sleep by the rhythm of waves.

Where else but Santa Barbara? The one place in California where mountains run east to west along the sea to leave a strip so narrow there's no land left for the ticky-tacky developers who gulped down my earlier home and spat out the Inland Empire.

Besides, I had a friend from junior high school and a couple of college pals who lived there. I flew out to check the emotional climate of several old folks' homes and instantly fell for Casa Dorinda. The Casa had been built by William Henry Bliss and his wife, Dorinda, beginning in 1916, in a spirit of adventure. As members of posh New York society, they envisaged a little country cottage in the wilds of the West.

They landed on forty acres of oak and redwood forest, with a creek running from La Cumbre Peak above to Butterfly Beach below. Here, Chumash people had pounded acorns and grilled fish for millennia. Here, Spaniards had planted olive trees, built tile-roofed missions, and raised cattle for centuries. Here, the Blisses would stake their claim to a new style by erecting a Spanish hacienda with Italianate touches overlooking the great lawn of an English manor house. Behold "Caliterannean."

I signed up instantly for the Casa's waiting list and put my New York apartment on the market. Now I could say goodbye to blinding columns of glass and steel, goodbye to the choking exhaust fumes at the corner of Seventh Avenue and Fourteenth Street as I fought my way up the subway stairs. I'd have to wait until they had a vacancy, but that would give me time to sell and clear out where I was.

That, however, became messy. In May, my ex-husband, Paul, by then living in Oregon, sorted out his life by dying. In September, I landed in the ER of Roosevelt Hospital with a transient ischemic attack, a ministroke. In October, Hurricane Sandy hit and flooded Lower Manhattan, and I was evacuated to the Upper West Side.

On November 4, I flew out on the first plane from Newark to Los Angeles and on to Santa Barbara. Two weeks later, the Cross-Country Moving Company truck limped into Santa Barbara with a load of broken boxes and missing jewelry.

NESTING

My *new home* at the old folks' home is a standard one-bedroom apartment, with a tiny kitchen and bathroom. I can't leave it alone. My first job is to remove the wall between kitchen and dining room so the space can open onto the extended patio, which borders on my coyote world. Even so, I'm not allowed to change the antiseptic color of the walls and floors, a visual embodiment of Casa decorum.

Instead, I create a nest of safety by covering the walls with paintings and drawings by my brother and daughter, and by my own high school self, mixed with photos that provide virtual protection from real fears. In the bedroom are more ritual fetishes, like the blue glass amulets I bought in Turkey. My four-poster bed is itself a fetish protected by the four Evangelists I point to, in order, while reciting "Matthew, Mark, Luke, and John, guard the ground I stand upon." So too is its coverlet, woven of thick mustard-colored yarn by descendant Mayas in Chiapas to keep the bogeyman away.

On the wall hanging above my bed, there's a blue Krishna dancing with his milkmaids amid a chorus of polka-dot cows. And above Krishna, the twin-horned head of the devil himself from Oaxaca, wearing a wreath of dried sandalwood flowers I'd been given when reporting on the World Vegetarian Congress in Bombay.

I look to these and other objects to keep me safe in my bed alone, once so crowded by three cats and a husband they seemed to be part of the bedding, like a quilt that both purred and snored. My real fear, however, is not from what is outside but from what is inside my room, inside myself. There is no protection from time. Witness my body.

On my arm, skin ripples over blue veins like the surface of a lake. A body I've known intimately for over half a century now seems entirely separate from myself, crinkling to its own rhythms, indifferent to good or evil.

MY DAY BEGINS

This morning, I woke up with Paul curled next to me. More than forty years since the last time we shared a bed—the beloved 1850 New England maple four-poster bed. But here he was, tucked into the narrow hospital-style bed I now sleep in, snoring as he always did. Hullo, Paul.

More and more I awake to dreams. Where am I? Who am I? When am I? Paul was there, but so was the memory that he died over a decade ago.

My kids and I learned of his death from the obits that poured in from British and American press alike. *The New York Times* wrote that the death of Paul Fussell was "the most profound tectonic shift in our literary culture in 2012." I like that phrase—*tectonic shift*—because the plates that make up Earth's crust suggest dinnerware and pies, and I've shifted plenty of both.

While we rejoiced in this outpouring of acclaim, we also struggled to find out just where, when, and how Paul had died, and where he had been buried.

I'd written my first memoir in "white fury" at the betrayal and loss of innocence in the face of war's realities in the battleground of the kitchen. My take was comic farce, appropriate to the weaponry of knives and forks and pie crusts. Paul never forgave me for writing about him, any more than he could forgive me for leaving him. He remarried in a flash, and I hadn't seen him for more than thirty years, although I knew I would always love him.

Alas, his death killed my movie fantasy of a deathbed reconciliation. It was no fantasy that his second wife had hated me long before she'd preceded Paul down the path of dementia to its inevitable conclusion.

But not before she'd estranged Paul from his own children and disinherited them by shifting their promised inheritance to her own children. The altered will and the power of attorney were now controlled by her son, who kept Paul's children off the contact list of the nursing home in Oregon to which he'd moved the elderly couple. This man eventually sent my children a small box of ashes along with some personal effects: a Purple Heart, twelve photos of Paul's parents, a college graduation robe, and two moth-eaten jackets.

Paul had always been a California beach boy, most at home stretched out on the sand with a book in front of his parents' summer cottage on Balboa Island. We spent many summers there and brought our kids to visit whenever we came out west. By May 2013, a year after Paul's death, I had finally landed in my unit in the old folks' home, and my kids arrived to visit, carrying that small box, ready to perform a ceremony of their own: a scattering of Paul's ashes in Balboa's Pacific blue.

While they were gone, I lit a candle in front of my two favorite photos of Paul: one as a laughing baby in bonnet and dress, the other as a teenager in his army uniform. I fell in love with the boy who would become the "war's laureate" when I was seventeen and he was twenty-one, a veteran looking for ways to express his "black fury" using the armor and sword of irony.

He'd enjoy the irony that today his legacy as a war writer has been superseded by his global presence gained via the website Magnificent Bastard, founded by those who regard his 1983 book, *Class: A Guide Through the American Status System*, as a kind of bible. "What would Fussell say?" is their secret handshake, the magic words for entrance to the club. That would make my kids and me honorary members, as we often imagine Paul's responses to follies both personal and national.

I look at him beside me, wavering now, as dreams do. Goodbye, Paul. Goodbye to his glory and his tragedy, the contradiction he embodied in remaining in that state of war for the rest of his life.

I don't need ashes to remind me of how he shaped my own life. His death is always less a tectonic shift than an ongoing tremor, as with Parkinson's, there to remind me of a Magnificent Bastard's power to shake lives with words.

MORNING RITES &
ABLUTIONS

Awake, I can't read the hands of a clock or watch, but I can tell from the quality of darkness how soon the dawn. When day coincides with clear sky, which is most of the time in Santa Barbara save the weeks of early-summer fog, the sun rises bright as a Meyer lemon through the long-limbed silhouette of my cedar tree.

In my old New York apartment, the sunlight entered obliquely through skylights. Here, a radiant halo filters through sunflowers, orchids, begonias, fuchsia. Flowers inside and out, a kaleidoscope of color. Time to face the day.

I spread my arms as wide as the tree. "Good morning, tree. Good morning, squirrels, birds, bees, bunnies." The cast of critters on my patio already scrabbling for breakfast. Hands on my waist now, thumbs to the rear, fingers front. A hug. "Good morning, liver."

Why liver? To honor Prometheus, his cycle of darkness and light. At sunset each day an eagle lands to devour the liver of the hero who stole fire from the sun to light our lives; and each night, his liver regenerates itself to bring the light back.

The morning ritual is exact and exacting. It's not my liver that needs regenerating, but the body entire, starting with the teeth. I still have most of mine, thank God. Most of the oldies I know keep their teeth in a cup of water. Toothpaste, toothbrush, two-minute scrub, up and down, up and down. Pray there's no pain. Pain means dentist, and that I'd rather avoid.

Next, pharmaceuticals. An exact sequence of steps, no improvisation allowed. Liquids first: drops into eyes, atomizers into mouth and nose. Then a bite of food: banana or yogurt preferred. Ten pills meted out in segmented dispenser, meant to be helpful if you can read what day it is on the lid of the container. If you even know what day it is. Pills for heart, lungs, stomach, skin, bones, bladder, gut, blood, nerves. Let's just say the general erosion of the body. And more pills for side effects from the initial round. Twice each day, every day.

Putting on the face. My public face, not the wrinkled ghost haunting my mirror. It's an act of fingertips and memory. Starting with a layer of sunscreen, applied religiously since I was in my thirties and had my first skin cancer removed. On top of that, a layer of matte-finish powder, a swipe of blush—color for the skull-pale skin. Eyebrow pencil to shade an approximation of the shape that used to be there; eyeliner for definition of eyes, necessary when lashes have mostly vanished too. A risk without clear vision might be an erratic expression of surprise I'm painting on myself, but better that than half a face. Finally, the lips. These are the hardest. Most of my friends retain to this day the shape and color of the lips they wore in high school. Lip liner, just enough to define a borderline, not too red. Then a muted shade on top.

That's the face for the day. It feels like an ordeal, but do it and you don't have to spend your time in front of a mirror depressed by the half face staring back at you. That's why the nurses in the med center are so attentive to their patients' appearances, even if they're just pushing them around in wheelchairs. Makeup was rightly seen as the flappers' declaration of independence.

And how lucky we gals are that we can put on costumes as well as masks to face the day. Decisions, decisions. Dress only once and you can save a lot of time. Check the weather. Waste time trying on different garments. Inspect for rips, tears, missing buttons.

You'll notice the shawl I picked out today. Isn't it pretty? A parting gift from my old friend Fleury, the last time I visited her in Princeton. She was an heiress of the agricultural Midwest when I first knew her, outgoing and generous. Now gone is the party-girl host of yore, her fire-hot love for friends, the sparkling bright champagne toasts and exorbitant buffets. When I saw her last, Fleury was bedridden, tended to by a full-time hospice nurse. She still wore her hair in a halo of orange and gold, but the focus of her blue-green eyes was elsewhere. In a rasping whisper not at all like the hoot and holler of her youthful voice, she told me to go to her closet and take anything I wanted. I demurred, but she commanded, "At least take some jewelry, then."

Fleury's jewelry was real, not the costume glitz and glamour that sparkled in my own chest. I picked out a pair of simple silver earrings. "Is that all?" she scolded. "What's the matter, you don't like my jewelry?" To assuage her, I chose another, similar pair that glimmered gold. "Don't worry," she said. "They're not 24-karat, just some kind of alloy."

On her, they would have looked like 24-karat, and the black hand-crocheted shawl she forced into my hands before leaving would have looked like Chanel. This is the Fleury I hear every day when I look in the closet. "You're not going to wear that tawdry old thing, are you?" she asks. "Here, take this. It's perfect for you."

I can't wait to show her that I've found the perfect party for her half-century-old crocheted shawl and faux-gold earrings. This is the perfect outfit for tonight's beast and feast. I think I can still smell a hint of Fleury's sexy perfume in the old threads.

WHY ARE OLD
MEN SO SAD?

And how lucky we gals are to learn at puberty that, primally, our bodies are our power. And to know that we can compensate for the erosions of time—a sag here, a thickening there—by a new bra or a looser blouse. Guys don't have it so good.

Of course, both sexes succumb to gravity, that telltale stoop of age as the head moves forward, heavy on the neck, as the spine slowly bends to let the head bob toward the belly, feet shuffling below. At breakfast, I watch the morning shuffle of silhouettes against the light of windows facing east, and I wonder: Why do I find the stoop and shuffle of old men so much sadder than that of women?

Is it because women learn so early the power of their bodies to attract, and adorn them accordingly, whereas men are stuck with the same stiff faces, shirts, and suits their fathers wore before them? It's true that men can choose to shave or not to shave, but otherwise male variants are few. And does it matter? Are their bodies beside the point? How many male power brokers owe their fame and glory to a great chest, a tight belly, and a full head of (real) hair? Even in our television age, with a male caricature posing in an orange comb-over, occupying the White House?

Women are luckier than men, even with our cultural fetish for youth. Over the decades women have watched first their pert nubbins swell—some a lot more than others—and learned how to keep them upright and forward-looking by cloth pulleys and straps, falsies, surgical implants, any size you want, to dazzle the flash of cameras. Despite all feminist rationalizations, gals know boobs & booties will always carry power. For men—nope. Good bodies are but a bonus to the aura of male power, the achievement of fame and glory by whatever means necessary. Wimpy bodies or fat bellies or bald heads or big spectacles no more detract from the power of a male celebrity than a white beard detracts from Santa Claus.

But at the breakfast table? Or shuffling to the bathroom? Loss of image is a loss of self for either gender, but maybe gals can pretend longer than guys that their self-image is intact—with a little help from hairdresser, manicurist, pedicurist, face lifter. But guys? They can tread on machines, or swim fifty laps a day, or lift twenty-pound barbells, but where's the rush that comes with racing to your board meeting? Your waiting staff in the operating room? Your opposing attorney in the courtroom? Where's the fun of winning? Where's the group of guys or gals who think, for that moment, you're God?

THE BREAKFAST CLUB

When I first arrived at the old folks' home, a little sign just visible through a window in the dining room commemorated a butter-yellow rosebush: *Planted by Julia Child's Breakfast Club.* Julia had left the club and the world at her death in 2004, but I was delighted to carry on the tradition. It was here, at the table beside the window beside the roses, that my group of friends gathered each morning. An intimate group that became family, in sickness and in health, till death do us part.

Which was frequent. Of the four original women who first joined me at the table by the rose window, none remain. The club iterated. New people came, old people went. By the time COVID hit, we were five, varying in age (seventy-seven to ninety-nine); gender (two guys, three gals); background (East Coast, West

Coast, Midwest); physical condition (three walkers, one oxygen tank); and character (reserved, flamboyant, sincere, playful). All five of us wore hearing aids, reading glasses, and sensible shoes. We were well educated and well traveled; we had led long, hardworking lives in the arts and sciences under the mores and manners established by twentieth-century upper-middle-class America. And, nearing the end of our lives, we had become all but invisible.

It was our peculiarities, not our geriatric genre, that drew us together. The oldest of us, stone-deaf but sharp of mind and sturdy of body, was as commonsensical as the nurse she'd been in World War II. Our youngest, a dandy who ran his own art gallery, declared himself gay after his divorce and relished sharing gossip with a wicked sense of humor. Next to him was a passionate lover of algae whose work had taken him around the world to teach and study marine biology, and whose curiosity had never ebbed. Our mother superior, frailest in body but strongest in mind, was a depth psychologist and coach whose two Mayo surgeon husbands had left her with wisdom and stories aplenty.

And then there was me, my native instinct to entertain or, some would say, to outrage. I thought of my role, though, as an enthusiast who longed to record every word on a secret tape recorder. Of course, I never did, but I often ambled back to my unit and wrote what I could remember of our oftentimes ludicrous dialogue:

"What's a Strawberry Moon?"

"I don't know. But we're supposed to have one visible at nine nineteen today."

"Never heard of it. What is it?"

"I dunno. Some kind of full moon."

"Did you see the moon last night? A little after nine o'clock?"

"No, I'm in bed by then."

"You think it's red?"

"What? No, I said *bed.* Not *red.*"

"The Strawberry Moon isn't red? You'd think it would be."

One of us takes out her iPhone and begins looking up Strawberry Moons.

"Did you hear Starbucks is going to start serving wine?"

"Starbucks? Oh, that's awful. I don't think I want wine with my coffee."

"You never go to Starbucks."

"Not now, but I used to, with my daughter."

"They sure made a success."

"I read they were bringing up the middle class."

"What does that mean?"

"'Starbucks is bringing up the middle class.' I got that from *The Atlantic.*"

"Up to where?"

"From where?"

Our Googler interrupts. She's found something on her iPhone.

"'Strawberry Moon' is what the Algonquians

called a full moon in June because it coincided with their large strawberry crop. Some European countries call it a Rose Moon."

"Well, since strawberries are California's biggest crop, we should have a Strawberry Moon at least once a year."

"If we could only see it through the fog."

"Oh look, there's some sunshine now. We're lucky."

"Nope, now it's gone."

"I like Starbucks coffee."

"We're drinking it now . . . I'm told that's where we get our coffee."

"Did you know David was missing yesterday?"

"Missing?"

"He'd moved himself into Personal Care, but they weren't ready for him, so they put him in Memory Care."

"Isn't his wife in Personal Care?"

"Yeah, and she was all ready to move into their new apartment there together, but he just jumped the gun and had friends move all his stuff in, but he hadn't gone through any of the proper channels."

"So where did he go when he was missing?"

"He got in his car and took off without telling anybody."

"Doesn't say much about Memory Care, does it? Or maybe too much."

"If there's a Strawberry Moon, what about the other fruits?"

EVERY DAY BUT SUNDAY

Breaking fast each day is as sacred a rite as the bread and wine of the Last Supper. The buffet table is a cornucopic testament to God's blessing. Fresh fruits and dried, wet oatmeal and dry cereals, yogurts, nuts, milks, sweeteners, breads for toasting, sweet rolls for sweet tooths, bacon and sausages, frittatas, scrambled eggs, hard-boiled eggs. Our table servers scuttle to fulfill our specific daily mantras, such as "A small glass of sugarless apple juice, half a buckwheat waffle very crisp, with melted butter and maple syrup, plus a small dish of applesauce with cinnamon, and a pot of hot water with one slice of lemon on the side."

Our wants are exacting. Details matter.

We are also self-selected early risers and take our same seats promptly between 7:30 and 7:35 a.m., with

28

apologies for lateness. Three leave by 8:15 for their daily exercise class of Balance & Strength in the former Activities Wing, now labeled Life Enrichment.

"No blueberries today."

"What? Again!"

If time rules the Casa, so do blueberries. So do flowers on the table. Fresh flowers. If ours look too wilted, we swipe better ones from a table not yet occupied.

Unfortunately, we cannot swipe better hearing from younger occupants, and we are fully aware of how ludicrous our conversations are. We laugh often and loudly.

We decide to organize a rhythm band.

As a youth, one of us had learned to play the glockenspiel. Another had always wanted to play the cymbals. A third had played the triangle once. The fourth offered to ring a bell. I volunteered to conduct. What we needed now was a piece devoted to these four instruments.

"Let's just take a familiar tune and compose our own orchestration. What about 'Home, Sweet Home'?"

"Or maybe 'Home Was Never Like This'?"

We agree that the Breakfast Rhythm Band is definitely our new project.

About once a week, one of us treats herself to an order from the kitchen for one slice of French toast, with one small container of melted butter and one of maple syrup, and two slices of bacon, very crisp.

When our server places the order before her, she says with shock, "There are bananas on my French toast. I didn't order that."

"Yes, you did."

"I did not! I ordered two strips of bacon very crisp."

"You said French toast and a banana. I'm sorry, I forgot the bacon."

"Not *sliced*! A whole banana to take home with me."

The server scurries to fetch a whole banana and two strips of very crisp bacon. Our resident scrapes the bananas off her toast while we sing in unison, "Yes, we have no bananas." Banana jokes should last us for weeks.

But our French-toast eater reinforces merriment the very next week when she again orders French toast. This time from one of our veteran servers who's worked at the Casa for decades.

"I'd like one slice of French toast with one small container of melted butter and one small container of mayo . . . mayo . . . nnaise . . . ?"

She falters, and we roar in unison, "*Syrup!*"

Our server joins us in creating other delicious variants on mayonnaise syrup, like Vermont mayo syrup? French mustard syrup? Poupon-mustard-and-mayo syrup for the pretentiously French?

Our youngest arrives late and sits down. "Freddie Feldman died."

"Did he have a heart attack?"

"He's a she. She fell *and* had a heart attack."

"I heard it was a blood clot, not heart."

"Isn't that heart? Part of circulation?"

"It counts as something else."

"Like what? What category is it under—like, who do you ask for if not a cardiologist?

"It's a vascular problem."

"You ask for a vascular surgeon?"

"A cardiovascular specialist. A problem in the veins and arteries."

"I heard they didn't find the body for quite a while."

"I heard that somebody in B building saw her fall."

"She lives right beneath me."

"Oh, I didn't know her."

"Didn't you hear those fire engines and the emergency ambulance?"

"Sure, but I didn't know who they were here for."

"Her heart attack could have caused the fall."

"Clot. Haven't they done an autopsy yet?"

"Dunno. Maybe they've done it, but we don't know the results."

"Anyway, she's dead."

"Better than living on in a wheelchair."

"Wait till it happens to you."

"How will I know if I'm dead?"

We move on to how our children or we as children first learned about sex.

"I had three older brothers and they told me everything—*every*thing."

"My daughter was sitting on her potty when she was three and looked down and said, 'Mama, I'm broken.'"

"My little son had just had a bath and held up his genitals in his hand and said, 'Mama, what are these balls for?'"

We move on to how our children handled death.

"When our son was told his grandpa was gone, he asked, 'Does *go* mean when you die you disappear?'"

"My daughter—who was precociously verbal and spoke in complete sentences at age two—is once again on her potty. 'Mama, what is it all for and why are we here?'"

That was the question we never voiced but all wanted answered.

SATURDAY SOUP OPERA

Food is a daily joy when you're old. There's more than breakfast to be savored in Santa Barbara. Every Saturday morning at 9:00 a.m. prompt, I go to the weekly farmers market downtown as if to church. The Casa van gives us exactly forty-five minutes to make our rounds, as ritualized as Stations of the Cross.

Fresh Juice Couple, selling liquid blood-orange, lemonade, pomegranate. Then Chris the Mussel Man, in crocheted hat hung with mussel shells, doling out mussels and sometimes oysters from the beds at Hope Ranch. "Hey, babe, give me some sugar!" he yells, asking for his weekly kiss.

Next the Raw-Butter Boy with a truckload of un-pasteurized milk, thick cream, fresh butter from the udders of happy cows who eat green grass. Nearby is the Olive Oil Man with local pressings flavored by rosemary, thyme, lavender. Not to mention the Lavender Lady with everything from fresh sprigs to oils, soaps, sachets. And on to Gaviota strawberries, heritage tomatoes, three varieties of avocado, passion fruits, cherimoyas, fresh gingerroot, multiple veggies, and greens waving their just-picked fronds.

Thank God, Elizabeth is still here at the Rancho San Julian stand, the ranch's beef having survived drought, floods, and fires. Her ancestors took up residence two centuries ago, when a former New Yorker named Thomas Dibblee married into the family of José de la Guerra, commander of Santa Barbara's Presidio and owner of a fourteen-thousand-acre Spanish land grant. The history of California is in each bite of pasture-fed flesh and marrowed bone.

All winter long, flowers bloom and perfume the air. Orchids of all colors and kinds, birds-of-paradise that grow like weeds. Van Gogh sunflowers, rainbow-colored gerberas, purple fuchsia, blood-red and salmon-pink begonias. I greet the Begonia Man, who'd arranged flowers for my niece's wedding over two decades ago. Everything here is personal.

At the market I use my walker as both grocery cart and aggressive tank to weave at full speed through crowded aisles, attempting to avoid baby strollers that claim right-of-way for their human cargo and malingering teenagers who stop midstream to chat. I play the old-lady card and shout "Beep beep!" I worry about losing my dark glasses when I peer closely at spots on this furry peach or feel up for ripeness that pebbled avocado.

My fingers fumble with crumpled bills, dropped coins, plastic bags that refuse to open. Since I lack one-dollar bills, I ignore the basket in front of the costumed lady who blows a long Tibetan horn. But I can't ignore the string band of elderly gents fiddling to entrance a group of tiny tots rooted in awe.

Home again, home again. To turn on Saturday morning's Met Opera broadcast on local station KUSC. I've been listening on Saturday mornings since I was six, when Milton Cross was my host on NBC. Today it's not from the Met live, but selected opera duets recorded by Pavarotti and Sutherland. I can relive their and my glory years at the opera house in New York while I prepare lunch in Santa Barbara.

Last week it was chicken broth because the Chicken Lady had not just innards but also chicken heads and claws. I like the way their beaked heads bobble on top of the boiling pot, seeming to sleep sweetly on a bed of claws. I always salvage a couple of claws so that I can nibble on their padded palms and knobby fingers, the soft, gelatinous texture of skin and flesh that tastes of bone.

Today I'll cook moules marinières. Machines have scrubbed those mussel shells spotlessly clean. I chop green garlic and scallions to soften in a pot with a pat of butter and a sprinkle of black pepper. I add water, or fish stock if I've got any, deep enough to cover the shells by an inch. When the water boils, in go the live mussels and on goes the lid. By now I'm exhausted, but the sun is high and my tray set with bowl, baguette, and a cold glass of Zaca Mesa Viognier from the fridge.

All is quiet on the patio but for a single hummingbird at the feeder and a few wasps. My opera duo has shifted to the "Miserere" at the end of *Il trovatore*, and I remember a San Francisco trattoria over half a century ago that surprised me with singing waiters. Leonora began her aria while serving me a hamburger, as her troubadour entered our crowded dining room from the men's room, rather than the kitchen. The voices of Pavarotti and Sutherland soar to climax as I raise my glass as chalice to thank the mussels for their sacrifice.

THE SEVERED HEAD

Remember Coyote, our shapeshifter? Always in the shadows, he reappeared as COVID in 2020, wreaking havoc on all our routines. We had to disband the breakfast club to practice appropriate social distance. I don't remember the last breakfast we had. We didn't know it was the last, although I'm sure we talked about the whispers of a deadly disease sweeping the world. But I'll always remember the yellow roses, the daily farce of misremembering and dismembering. We were more than one another's shared security blanket. Sure, we'd always send an email when we knew we'd be absent from breakfast, to make sure none of us would think we were dead in bed. And what was said at the breakfast table stayed at the breakfast table, because we were guaranteed to forget it. Or to mishear it to begin with. But the most important thing was the fact that we saw one another every single day because we cared.

The pandemic devoured our communal breakfast ritual and left us to eat, as we did everything else, in total isolation. Every meal, a masked employee would leave a tray at the door with whatever I'd ordered the night before. Like prison in the movies, but with more food.

But eating alone's no good for anyone, and especially not for me. So I took to the company of the critters on my patio, eating outside in the warming sunlight while birds and squirrels pecked at the ground around my feet, begging for crumbs. "Don't be greedy, I've already fed you," I said. Every morning, the same game. I'd throw a pile of seed at 8:00 a.m. on the dot, and they'd all scrabble to steal their portion. Then, just as quickly as the seed was gone, they'd forget they'd ever eaten it at all, so by the time I sat at the patio table to eat, they were starving again.

I hear some workmen passing below my terrace and giggling. I notice that my proud papa plant of pot is thriving, stretching his green arms out even farther than before. A friend from Ojai had brought him with strict instructions on what he needed to grow—a full shower twice a day and full sun all day. I even moved him to a sunnier corner when management with embarrassment warned me that there'd been resident complaints about his exposing himself along my fence. But he was legal, for heaven's sake, and sorry to say, impotent through no fault of his own. Without a mama plant, his juvenescent powers to fertilize were nil. But I loved him because he was so proud and bore himself like a man.

Suddenly, a strange shape on the ground catches my eye. A small wad covered with tiny ants. I peer closer, pick it up with my spoon, wondering if it is a baby bird fallen from the nest. I hold it as close to my eyes as I dare with the ants swarming around. Not feathers, but fur. Strange. Not a beak, but four curved teeth like a beaver's, only thinner and longer.

It has to be a squirrel, or a gopher, but what kind of predator severs the head and leaves it behind? Was it for me, some kind of hunter's gift? It's true, I used to gnaw on chicken heads that I got from the market to use for stock, but a rodent head? No way.

I'm sitting in sheer puzzlement with the spoon poised in front of my face when the phone inside rings, startling me into dropping the head with a small, crunchy *thwack* on the ground. I run inside to answer.

"Are you Betty Fussell?" asks a male voice. Older, I think.

"I am."

"I'm Bob," he says. "I'm an advanced obituary writer from *The New York Times*. I've been assigned to you."

I shriek, and the birds outside scatter in a flurry of feathers. "I'm going to make the *Times*? I can't believe it. Best news I've had in thirty years." After this stunner of an opening, all of Bob's subsequent fact-checking feels almost annoying.

Then I begin to worry. Is this a scam? Bob is getting all of my personal info. "Were your parents known by their middle names, Meryl and Hazel, instead of Josias and Ruby?" Good Lord, was my mother's first name really Ruby? At least Bob hadn't yet asked for my Social Security number.

He assures me he's written for the *Times* for decades, working his way up from copyboy to Pulitzer Prize winner. I Google him while he talks and read his latest obit, which happens to be for an old Princeton friend of mine whom I didn't realize had died.

After he's extracted all the data, Bob hangs up, and I click through a few more of his obits. I have to admit, he is a good writer. But does he know something? Was the severed head some kind of sign? Should I check my directives, make sure the will is up-to-date, make sure I've signed that DNR? Surely it's Coyote leaving the severed head behind. A way of saying he'll be back. He must have notified Bob the obit writer too. One of those cosmic invites.

I add to my morning prayers: Dear God, please do not let the Pope or King Charles or any major movie star or musician die at the same time as me. Just give me two inches, Lord, and no misspellings.

COYOTE PIE
Making the Crust

Now, *dear reader*, I'm not done telling the story yet, but even half blind, I can see you're looking hungrier by the minute. Was that you I heard, sniffing, your nose turned to the blossoming smell of Coyote Pie wafting through the kitchen? Yes, it surely smells delicious. And I haven't brought you all this way to leave you without a recipe. So let me walk you through it. Because someday, no matter how you feel about it, no matter what you do or don't do, no matter how far you run or how well you hide, Coyote's coming for you too. May as well learn how to cook him up into something tasty before he gets there.

We'll start with the crust, our sacramental bread. Now, the crust seems simple, but it's as important as the filling. Get it wrong, and you've got insides

41

bubbling right through to the side of the pan. A total mess, in other words. Or worse, a crust that's tough and dry as old cardboard.

Get the best cornmeal you can find, preferably freshly ground. That means ordering from a good company online, unless you happen to grow your own corn and grind its kernels with an old-fashioned mortar and pestle. Or know someone who does.

Of course, there's always the supermarket cornmeal. Instant grits and the like save you mountains of time and effort. But if you use them, do not seek forgiveness from the corn goddess for diminishing the texture and flavor of the meal.

You may also have trouble finding fresh lard at the grocer's. You can replace it with bacon fat or, if it comes to it, butter.

INGREDIENTS
3 cups cornmeal grits, cooked
3 cups meat broth
¼ pound of fresh lard, softened
Salt and pepper, to taste

INSTRUCTIONS
In a large bowl, stir the grits and broth. Gradually whip in the fat until the mixture is light and airy. Add salt and pepper. Cover and set aside in a cool place while you make the filling.

HOW NOT TO HUNT
A COYOTE

Now that we've prepped the crust, let's take a break.
Sit back down, have a coffee. I know you'll be want-
ing the recipe for the filling, but first I have to tell
you a little more about Coyote. After all, I'd known
him well long before the severed head arrived at my
patio. Coyote the trickster, Coyote the fire starter,
Coyote the joker pranking himself. I'd gobbled up
as many myths as I could find.

And the more I learned about Coyote, the more I
wanted to meet him, live, in the wild where he lived.
So I was delighted when my son, Sam, invited me to
his cabin in Montana for Thanksgiving. He lives in
one of the coldest spots in America, near the foot of
Glacier National Park, and he promised to show me
how to hunt coyotes in the snow.

I'd visited earlier in life, a mere eighty-five years

old, so that Sam could show me how to hunt a deer. It was springtime then, so the weather was good, and at that time I was only half blind. I'd never held a gun, but I wanted to enter my son's world. I wanted to know what it felt like to move from grad school at Oxford, to a body-building career in New York and L.A., to distance motorcycling from Nome to Key West, to underwater rescue and recovery diving in the lakes of Montana, to, now, an off-grid cabin in Montana, where he became a full-time mountain man.

Hunting with Sam, I bonded with the wild in a way I never expected. The white-tailed doe that I shot lives with me now and forever. Her flesh became my own when I ate her heart that night for dinner, and her muscle as steaks and sausages for over a year. Her furred skin and skull on my wall remind me daily of my debt. Her life for mine.

But the coyote, unlike the deer, gets no respect dead or alive. As Mark Twain wrote, "The coyote is a long, slim, sick and sorry-looking skeleton . . . a living, breathing allegory of Want." Government wildlife agencies require no license to shoot coyotes since they are classified as "predators and varmints." In fact, wildlife agencies promote sterilization, trapping, poisoning, and even germ warfare to get rid of these varmints to the tune of half a million each year.

After watching hours of videos on hunting coyotes, Sam handed me my gun, and the muzzle immediately fell to the ground, too heavy for me to hold. Sam would have to carry my gun, as well as his own and, as it turned out, *me*.

Since coyotes are keen sniffers, Sam was fanatic about removing all human scent from our bodies. For five days our routine was rigid. Breakfast at 4:00 a.m. Shower with no soap. First layer of long johns, thermal socks, and boots. Stagger outside in the snow to a pine-burning smoke pit. Stand front-side then backside to smoke each layer of clothing, beginning with base layer, then fleece pants, shirt, sweater, jacket, balaclava, beanie, gloves, mittens, hat, scarf, coat.

Then we'd drive up the mountain to the same spot, a logging trail near where I'd shot my deer. Since new snow had deceptively masked the thick ice beneath, I tried to walk precisely in Sam's foot-steps as he crunched ahead, pointing to prints and scat of coyote, buck, bobcat, wolf, black bear, grizzly.

We crawled over a series of branches and rocks to find the blind Sam had built, a sniper's nest with a stump for a backrest. Sam set up a rabbit decoy fifty yards from our hiding spot, and when he clicks a remote, the bunny wiggles his ears and Sam whistles through his hands to mimic the sounds of a cotton-tail in distress. We are on high alert. No sound, no motion, eyes fixed beneath the scope of our rifles.

A sudden whoosh above our heads sends off a flurry of snow from the tree. Gigantic wings and tal-ons scrape the top of our blind. Sam's call has lured a great gray owl to our distressed cottontail. Sam is elated. I'm scared. For the next four hours, nothing happens. I keep hallucinating the golden eyes and pointy ears of a coyote where there are none. As dawn lightens the dark, Sam motions that it's time to go home, empty-handed.

Once again I follow in Sam's footsteps. He slips, falls, and picks himself up, and I follow on to the same place, where I slip, fall, and stay put. I hear my right ankle snap, and I'm sure I've broken it. Sam slings me over his shoulders like a bear carcass and lugs me down the path to his Jeep. The nearest emergency room is in Kalispell, two hours away. Because it's Thanksgiving Day, we sit in the waiting room for another three hours while I bite my tongue to keep from yelling in pain. No nurse will give me so much as an aspirin without a doctor. No doctor wants to leave his turkey dinner for a near-empty ER in Kalispell.

When a doc finally arrives to examine my ankle, he determines it wasn't bone but ligament that snapped. At each touch of his hands I scream loudly. When he has to position my ankle for the X-ray, I hold on to Sam's arm and bite hard. Once we get home, Sam bares his arm to show me my toothmarks.

"Nobody told me you'd bite," he said, shocked.

"That's what they do in the movies," I reply.

I didn't get to meet my ghost dog, not even his shadow, but I know he was out there. Somewhere. Waiting for me as I wait for him now, half a smile and half a leer. We both know it's just a matter of time.

HOW NOT TO COOK
A COYOTE

The summer following my disastrous coyote hunt, once my ankle had finally healed up enough to hobble around with a cane, I traveled to Mexico with my daughter, Tucky. Our rental, a repeat for many years, was a cottage called Casa Temictli on a cobblestone street called Nezahualcóyotl in a village called Tepoztlán. My Lord, those Nahuatl names! I can't even speak Spanish properly, let alone this indigenous Aztec tongue.

Luckily, I didn't have to, since Tucky's very skilled in languages. Skilled enough to get a translation for me: we stayed in the House of Dreams, on the street of the Coyote Who Fasts, in the village of Copper Axe Above a Hill.

Those rugged cliffs with ruins that loomed above the village were deemed the birthplace of the creator god, Huehuecóyotl. What I didn't know was that Coyote had chosen to take out his revenge for my attempted hunt, turning our House of Dreams into a House of Nightmares.

From the minute we arrived, my spine began to protest the shuffling, cobblestoned, cane-limping footsteps I was forced to take. I took to sleeping downstairs on a sofa rather than braving the stairs to get to kitchen and bath. One night, Tucky left to visit old friends, a family we'd been close to, but I stayed home, too tired to do anything but turn on the World Cup soccer game.

Suddenly, I heard a groan from within my lungs, and my pulse stampeded like hooves on stone. I couldn't breathe. I felt like I was suffocating, imploding at high altitude. Outside, a flash of lightning, a blast of thunder, and then all the lights went out. Total power outage. The Aztec lightning god, Xolotl, speaking directly to me.

I fumbled in the dark for my cell phone and, with some luck, managed to dial Tucky and beg her to return. "I can't breathe," I said. "I'm imploding, and it's too dark to see anything." Within ten minutes, I heard the sound of a car pulling up outside. It was well past midnight, but the whole family had joined my daughter to drive me to the hospital. Somehow, over a series of agonizing hours, the doctors lowered my blood pressure and stabilized my breathing. Eventually, they sent me back to the street of the

Coyote Who Fasts. Or, more simply translated, the Hungry Coyote.

I woke the next day with a migraine and a back spasm that I knew immediately would neither be calmed nor cured. I was as helpless as our miracle firstborn, who entered the world howling and didn't stop for three years. Our doctor called it colic, but I knew she just had common sense. In Mexico, we reversed roles. Now it was my daughter who longed to comfort and felt helpless to do so. There's no comfort for some kinds of pain. She brought ice packs and soup, and I told her that if I was going to die, I'd like to die in my own language.

So we flew out the next day, Tucky to her new teaching job in India and me to my old folks' home in California. I knew it was our last time in Tepoztlán together. But not our last time ever. And I saw, after all this time, how much my children were like each other. My daughter sought the wild in new places, new people, new languages; her brother sought the wild by calling it to his place, his home, his language. Both hungered for the intensity of experience and feasted on every moment that arrived. I'd bonded with my son by following his footsteps to hunt for a coyote. With my daughter, I'd bonded by drinking a cup of hot soup under the all-seeing eye of the creator god, Huehuecóyotl, Very Old Coyote.

Descendants of European culture, like me, are trained from birth to think and feel in binary ways.

Either/Or. Good/Evil. Life/Death. A universe built of conflict. Far more ancient cultures saw it differently. Connection is key. Union. Huehuecóyotl, unlike strict and stodgy creator gods of other cultures, is the life of the party. He dances up a storm covered in bird feathers from coyote head to human toe, loudly singing and celebrating the union of sky and earth, of sex and death, of metamorphosis and mischief-making.

Coyote by any name knows in his ancestral bones that death is as vital to life as fasting to feasting. Curiously, the Coyote Who Fasts was not just the name of our street in Mexico but also the name of a real human being. Nezahualcóyotl ruled Tepoztlán forty years before Cortés arrived from Spain in 1519 to slaughter Montezuma and take over the New World. As a ruler, Nezahualcóyotl was famed for both his piety and his poetry, celebrating in daily rituals the circle of day and night, sun and moon, summer and winter, imaged by the circular open jaw of the jaguar. Fasting Coyote knew then what we try to forget even today: that no matter what we prepare for dinner, we are the goose that's cooked and eaten.

COYOTE COMES TO
THE CASA

"*Did you see* a dog this morning by the dining hall?"
one of the residents asks.

"You mean that coyote?" I didn't see it, but I did
read the announcement the Casa emailed to all residents warning of coyote sightings, advising: *Do not
approach. Make loud noises. Do not run. Back slowly and
calmly away.*

She's shocked. She's never seen a live coyote
before.

"Did it have big pointy ears like a fox and gray
hair like a wolf?" I ask.

"Maybe . . ." She's cautious. She's never seen a fox
or a wolf either. Or maybe she's just afraid.

I often hear coyotes singing in the hills to the
north and once in a while I see one skulking through
the oak grove. But I am lucky enough to look at my

own coyote pelt every day, stretched out nose to tail along a chair in my living room. He'd been a 'yote in his prime, thick winter coat of whitish gray and beige. Right at home surrounded by a collection of skins and skulls and feathers sent over the years from my hunter son, Sam, in Montana. Gifts, all of them, and remembrance of the life/death cycle we are all a part of.

Floods, fires, and a debris slide had long ago tarnished the vision of a benevolent Mother Nature, yet our fantasy of control remains. The Casa advertises itself as a place of "refinement and enhanced living," where people never die but instead "depart" or "pass on." Hedges are sculpted, lawns are manicured, not a flower wilts that isn't promptly clipped away.

But night is falling quickly. There's no illusion about it. The day passes on. Coyote or dog, the wild that lurks like a shadow comes closer.

Do not run. Back slowly and calmly away.

COYOTE PIE
Making the Filling

That pie in the oven has real coyote meat. Smell it? The perfume of nighttime and trickery. Yes, it makes me smile too. What a wide smile you have, dear reader. But I know what you're thinking: no, it isn't coyote from these parts. Sourcing coyote meat's no easy feat. Plenty of coyotes get hunted, but few hunters are willing to scrape out the tough, stringy meat. My meat came courtesy of a friend in the Hudson Valley. Their coyotes eat the deer that eat the plants of the valley farmers, driving them nuts. This meat, therefore, tastes like venison. Predators taste like what they eat. Coyote meat from these parts of California would taste of rabbit and gopher and coyote berry. If it had snuck into some gated backyard, maybe a hint of small dog or cat. So what fills the pie is coyote, but also, what filled the coyote. Such is our feast.

INGREDIENTS
3 tablespoons olive oil
1 large white onion, chopped
2 garlic cloves, chopped
1 green bell pepper (or ½ seeded jalapeño or poblano pepper)
4 cups shredded coyote meat, braised
2 pimento peppers, chopped
1 ½ cups pitted olives
4–6 tablespoons chili powder, chili adobo, or chipotle chili, to taste
Salt and pepper, to taste

INSTRUCTIONS
In a large frying pan, heat the oil before adding the onion, garlic, and green pepper. Sauté until slightly browned, about five minutes, then add the braised meat and mix well. Add the pimentos, olives, and spices and cook until the mixture is heated through. Taste and adjust as needed. Remember, the cornmeal crust will balance much of the chili's heat.

Coyote likes a bit of spice. Coyote's flesh is stringy and tough. You have to boil it for a few hours to soften it enough to be edible. In itself it's tasteless.

People have been the filling of the pie of my life. They give it the juice, the flavor, the spice, the sweet and the savory. The people in my life are the essential condiments and spices.

BROTHER BOB

It's never been my own epitaph that's occupied me quite as much as the ones I'd write for the people who meant the most to me. Most of them are gone by now.

Gone, but not forgotten. Starting earliest in life with my brother, Bob. Four years older than me, and from my birth a boy I both feared and adored.

Bob quit high school and left home without warning. He got a friend to drive him down to San Pedro. Lied about his real age, seventeen, to enlist. A month later, Pearl Harbor was bombed, and Private Bob Harper shipped out to Guadalcanal. "We fell like ducks in a shooting gallery," he told me later, showing me a series of sheets of his drawings he'd kept as a kind of war diary when he was hospitalized in the service.

My brother had a lifelong passion for airplanes that I date to a summer vacation in Long Beach, 1932, when Dad treated us to a ten-minute ride on a monoplane. I was five, Bob was nine. It was the one-buck thrill of a lifetime until the pilot looped upside down in the roofless plane, and I discovered my seatbelt was useless. I clung to Bob like my life depended upon him, which it did. All the while, he hooted with joy. And because I loved my brother, I loved airplanes for the rest of my life too.

Bob gave up his dreams of being a pilot to care for his wife and two kids, and I left my husband to travel the world. By fifty, he suffered from emphysema, and by sixty, his wife had deteriorated into Alzheimer's. I called him when I could, asked how he was doing.

"Oh, I'm getting by," he'd say, wheezing over the phone. Short sentences only. "Been to the hospital twice. It's the breathing. Half blind now too. Still drive, though. I'm surviving."

After his wife died, Bob became a prime target for lonely widows who wanted to comfort a wounded war hero but were less interested in his family. His second wife moved him from the altar to Tennessee, where she insisted he focus solely on her. No room for his past, for anything he'd lived or loved before her.

Despite her protests, I visited Bob there as a surprise, bringing our first cousin, Charles, along. My brother was fully bedridden by then, hooked up to an oxygen tank. He seemed happy to see us, but his wife kept us from talking alone with him with the excuse that memories of the past upset him.

Charles and I were more cunning, though. I distracted her in the kitchen while Charles snuck to his bedside. Bob came to life, Charles told me later. He just needed another guy to talk to, to relive the old days.

Bob died not long after our visit, just before his eightieth birthday. We didn't hear anything from his wife, and only she knew where he was buried. I tried to find those drawings, the war diary from Bob's days on Guadalcanal. I learned his wife had burned them in the fireplace to keep him safe from any memories of the past that didn't include her. Ashes to ash.

I feel Bob's presence most in the house his son built in San Diego, on a hillside terrace with a glimpse of the sea. There my brother's spirit flies in a plane, cloud to cloud, his paintings still hanging on his kids' and grandkids' walls, unchanged.

MY BEST FRIEND, PAT

Family's like raw meat—largely unpalatable without the seasoning of close friendships. All my life I've counted on friends to construct the family I lacked. Pat, my best friend since junior high school in Riverside, was like a sister to me. Seventy years of friendship. I miss her and don't miss her, because she's gone and not gone. Her ashes are in a vial around the neck of that clay jaguar on my fireplace mantel. Got him in a village near Chiapas in Mexico and flew him back cradled in my lap. Pat is always there, on the neck of that jaguar, and here, in my heart.

Particular foods always remind me of particular friends, and with Pat, it's French fries and beer. As an adolescent I could never afford French fries, and in my house beer was forbidden. Even Coca-Cola was forbidden. Pretty much everything fun was forbidden. So when I met Pat, she was as exotic as Wonder Woman. She'd been born in Cyprus (wherever that was) and raised in Elmira (wherever that was) by her granny, since her parents were always off to foreign parts. When they dropped by to visit from time to time, they smoked and drank and threw wild parties like people in the movies. Glamorous and unreal.

Pat and I were aliens in a town of the stiff and proper. She could cross her eyes and stretch her mouth into any wild expression, a slapstick Alfalfa to my straight-man Shirley Temple. We were a regular comedy team, Harper and Sides. So much so that we regularly wrote, directed, and starred in our own musicals.

Come high school, Pat was the first girl I knew to drive her very own Ford pickup truck. Bright red, of course. She drove us to school and to the theater, but also to drive-ins to smoke and drink beer and eat fries. I didn't dare smoke or drink, but I sure loved the fries. Naturally, my parents forbade me to see her, but there was no stopping us.

We plotted to attend Pomona College together and live in the same dorm, and when the wartime gas rations threatened to put a damper on our fun and adventures in the old Ford truck, Pat stuck out her thumb and hitchhiked. Nothing could stop her. And nothing kept her from taking me along for the ride.

Nothing except, of course, the return of the war

veterans to campus. One by one, our friends turned boyfriends into lovers into husbands. We watched them star in their own romances and giggled like adolescents. Even around me, Pat had always shut the door on conversations about any emotional or personal intimacy. Maybe clowning was a mask to hide her fear of both.

And maybe it isn't so odd that the war veteran I eventually fell in love with wore much the same mask, but his was built of irony instead of humor. Nor is it odd that Pat never married. Instead, she became a high-powered career gal in New York City. She was the first person I knew to embark on the great adventure of television in the fifties. She wrote, directed, and produced for PBS, CBS, ABC; traveled the world in search of stories and interviews; and lived in a studio on the Upper East Side with a succession of rescued border collies, the real loves of her life.

When I returned to Manhattan post-divorce, we revived the old Harper-Sides lust for performance. But in the competitive worlds of television and life alike, the young were nipping at our heels. Pat fought the facts of time as stubbornly as she'd lived the rest of her life. I spent twenty years in wonderment at her utter denial that old age or death could happen to her or to anyone she loved.

Like my brother, when Pat was diagnosed with emphysema, she refused to cut back on her pack-a-day. She was skeletal-thin and increasingly attached to an oxygen tank, but she still lit up a Kool and kept me at bay. "I'm fine," she'd say. "Mari's taking care of me." Mari, a young gal who'd apprenticed with Pat on TV and served now as dog walker, caretaker, and stage manager for Pat's closing number, called me often about taking Pat to the ER. The cancer chain had begun. Ovarian, breast, then liver.

I went to visit her once. "I'm fine," Pat said, lighting up a Kool. "Look at this great view of the East River." All I saw was a skull. All bone, hollow eye sockets, lips withdrawn, hair wispy, skin ashen. As I left, I heard Mari weeping. "I'll do anything for you, Pat," Mari said. "Just tell me what to do."

"Will you trade places with me?" Pat said.

That night I dreamt that Pat and I were at an amusement park in front of a ride that headed into a tunnel. I was fumbling for our tickets when the tunnel entrance shut. Pat was gone. "Where'd she go?" I asked the cashier, who then vanished too. I woke up in a panic. I knew Pat was gone, for good.

But not her words and not the playbills and videos that I had to pack up into boxes as I prepared for a last move. She resisted time, fought death, but no matter her take, she taught me a different way to greet Coyote.

PRINKLE THE ELF

She was Prinkle to my Flossie, and we wrote letters as these characters for over sixty years while we lived parallel lives in overlapping places. I was the Tall One, she the Tiny, so I thought of her as my Elf Self, born in Southern California the same year as me, with the same need to explore the wide world of Words and Images.

She twinkled around our college campus like Puck on steroids, quoting Gertrude Stein, Matisse, Picasso, names unknown to most of us. While my usual Girl Gang was out cheering our football team, she was sketching caricatures of the players, the cheerleaders, us. She lived to draw, paint, design, and so she did, until her final breath at eighty-nine in a rest home in Santa Cruz near her son.

Today my walls in Santa Barbara are as alive

with her paintings and drawings as they were in Princeton and New York. I wish you could see them now, especially the big canvas that hangs above my mantel, which is like a painted selfie. We'd hung so many Prinkle paintings in our Princeton house that we asked her to parody the genre of the Artist in His Studio. By weird coincidence, the physical fireplace mantels in my last three living rooms have been identical. So are the Prinkle paintings that surround it. Relatively new is the abstract collage Prinkle created the year before she died, frail in both body and memory, but not in perception or skill.

Prinkle had left college after her sophomore year because she was ready for the world, first San Francisco and then New York. In San Francisco she fell in love with Charlie, a man ten years older who ran a frame shop and managed jazz player Turk Murphy. "Charlie was the Big Romance," she told me later, "but I was a young thing, and it didn't mean the same thing to him."

She moved straight on to the Big City we all yearned for, where she launched her career as a well-paid commercial artist and illustrator of interiors for magazines. In New York she met Al, a designer of furniture and interiors of German Danish extraction, who loved sailing and his house on Long Island.

I followed in Prinkle's tiny footsteps when I fled to San Francisco after college, and then finally to New York. Prinkle was there to show me the ropes:

where to go to get beer by the schooner, to hear the best jazz, to get the best discount for MoMA.

We both got married about the same time, she to a visual artist, me to a verbal one. While I moved to Boston and New London, she moved to Long Island. In a few years we produced progeny about the same time, and for the next decades we traveled widely abroad without ever crossing paths.

No matter. She was as assiduous in her letter writing as in her drawing, and I wish I could show you the boxes and boxes of letters in her wondrous calligraphic hand that I gave to her son after her death.

Oddly enough, we even *left* our husbands about the same time in the eighties and without consultation rented Village apartments on Ninth Street near Fifth Avenue two doors from each other. We discovered that for strangely similar reasons we lived in the same odd limbo of loving our longtime mates while finding them impossible to live with.

But it wasn't long before she moved back to San Francisco and Charlie. "I've been in love with Charlie forever," she said. "Then we each got married to other people, and I'm so structured, you see, I just built a structure around him in my head and put him in and kept him there all these years. And after his wife died, we just picked up where we'd left off because for me nothing had changed."

Except for Charlie's frame shop, which had become the Charles Campbell Gallery, famous for the works of once-struggling artist pals now modern masters like Wayne Thiebaud and Richard Diebenkorn. Charlie's eye was as sharp and adventurous as Prinkle's in spotting gems where others saw haystacks.

Whenever I visited San Francisco as a journalist, I would visit the gem they'd created on Potrero Hill, in a tiny house and yard where the views inside were as staggering as out. Outside swept the glittering skyscrapers of the city, the bay, the Oakland hills. Inside condensed the world's arts and crafts in miniature, every inch of every room crammed floor to ceiling.

From Prinkle I learned the art of treasuring for itself every item of her daily life—whether toothbrush, pot, broom, bowl of pansies, linen napkin. From Charlie I learned the art of juxtaposition: a Balthus drawing next to a pre-Columbian god in clay.

For me, Prinkle and Don Carlos (as I called him) were a magic couple, undeterred by his last decades of blindness from macular degeneration. Prinkle even learned to drive a car to help serve as guide dog until his death at ninety-nine. I was lucky enough to attend his wild ninetieth birthday party in a wharf warehouse at North Beach packed with what seemed to be hundreds of friends. We all, especially the birthday boy, jitterbugged until dawn to the jazz trumpets of the survivors of Turk Murphy's band.

CHARLOTTE'S WEB

There she is, on my Wall of Fame, staring straight at me in this black-and-white senior photo of a Princeton High School graduate of 1941. I stare back at three strings of pearls and curly hair above the naked shoulders of her décolletage. But what about those straight-arrow brows and eyes that nail you to the wall? And that Cupid's-bow mouth, with its hint of smile or smirk, an echo of Becky Sharp in *Vanity Fair*?

Ask her four husbands, but they're gone. I met her in the sixties after her first divorce from a university professor to raise three children on her own while pursuing her career as an actress. Look, here she is in the next photo, playing Ariel in *The Tempest.* And who has posed for the camera in the Princeton Players' lineup of the cast but Albert Einstein, a fan

who never missed a show on campus. He'd died by
the time we hit Princeton and learned that the female star of the Players lived in the street behind us.

The next picture is Charlotte at her wedding reception dancing with her second groom, Edward, a
Princeton philosophy professor. I'm there dancing
with my husband. We gals are in long dresses, me in
a picture hat speaking over my husband's shoulder
to Charlotte. My lips are distorted as if saying the
F-word, but more likely *fun* than *fuck*.

Both describe the days when, as Charlotte said,
"Fucking itself was fun." Charlotte in real life talked
like an Irish washerwoman whose accent was over-
laid with the intonations of Queen Mary, consort to
George V. Charlotte's washerwoman voice was more
fun than any I'd ever heard, and I scrambled to
write down her words verbatim whenever we talked
by phone, which was often, after I moved to New
York.

About six months after I'd left my husband,
Charlotte called from Princeton in a voice omi-
nously low and soft.

"I must be the biggest jackass in the world," said
Charlotte. "I couldn't tell you before, but Ed and
I are separating. There's another woman—in England, all that time he spent pretending to research
his damn Wittgenstein. I must have been blind,
deaf, and dumb. I saw on his desk an American
Express seven-hundred-and-fifty-nine-dollar phone
bill, and suddenly I knew. 'This was for Annabel,

wasn't it?' I asked. He said, 'Yes,' and confessed the whole affair. He wondered why I was so calm. 'I'm not mad at all,' I said, 'I'm perfectly calm.'"

Listening to Charlotte was better than a movie. She told me Ed met Annabel when he was a Jewish refugee from Berlin to London and she a Wasp from Yorkshire.

Charlotte went on: "'We were wrong from the start,' he says. He didn't say that when he asked me to raise his two young boys and I did. Now he's in a dilemma, he says, because he loves me and loves her and doesn't know what to do. He *wants* to suffer, to agonize over everything. But I'm not angry. I'm cool."

A week later she called me after Ed had moved to a motel.

"It's so sneaky. That's what I can't get over. Now it all comes tumbling out. He blames me for everything, wants a new life, wants to be free, move to England, where he and Annabel can retrace the paths that once they trod and find the haystacks where they tumbled. For the first time I really believe I could kill him.

"Did you know that his first wife was killed by a speeding truck on V-J Day when he was on a troop ship coming back from Europe? And his second wife went crazy after an elephant in a zoo killed their two-year-old baby when they got too close. Now it seems it was all my fault.

"I mean, darling, I am a Medea who doesn't need to kill children; I'm just going to kill *him*."

She warmed to the magnificence of her performance.

"I've got him by the short and curlies. I surprised myself when I did go out of control. Medea in comparison was Kate Greenaway. You didn't hear me shrieking? You thought that was a wild boar being slaughtered in the hills? Wrong. That was me across the Hudson in New Jersey. I tell you the phones rattled and fell to the floor. You never heard such a shriek.

"But I do feel sorry for him. He wants to come home, says he adores me. I told him, 'It's over, Harry, over. Don't come sniveling back to *my house*.' I missed a stage performance that night for the first and only time in my life. Drank a full bottle of vodka and vomited for eight hours straight and had to call in sick."

She checked back with me at the end of the summer.

"I don't feel anything about Edward. After two days of total rage, I'm absolutely numb. I hope I'm getting over this terrible sense of failure, that I married a piece of shit. Marriage is impossible. How can anybody stay married? It's too hard now. There aren't any rules."

Two weeks later she called roaring with laughter. That was good because I knew she'd been helicoptered to a hospital in Philadelphia after a heart attack, from which she'd now evidently recovered.

"She died in November, Annabel did, after a long bout with cancer. Isn't that a laugh? And Edward didn't go because he heard about it too late."

71

Charlotte's period as a grass widow was not lengthy but long enough to concern her. "My shrink keeps talking about eligible men. She's off her rocker. Has she been out there on the street? How dare she tell me to get out and sell myself? To *whom*? I feel lucky if they've got two arms and two legs, forget the penis."

Her current consolation was a man she'd met in the Philadelphia hospital.

"He's been fabulous, but I think it's over. I mean, he's very vital for seventy, but he is frail. How can he help it at that age? Did I mention he's Black? And he thinks I'm a child. *He thinks I'm beautiful.* I'm terrified he'll find out I'm not, but darling, with him I am. He's my good friend and lover, and he's out of the hospital now, so I see him once a week. But I won't play nursemaid."

A few months later Charlotte celebrated her sixtieth birthday at a huge party given by her closest friends, Louise and husband William, in their huge house in the oldest of the old-rich part of town.

"I'm so hung over all I want to do is drown. Haven't even brushed my teeth or washed my crotch. Maybe a little booze both places, you think? I don't remember going to bed last night. God, I look like everybody's granny. Too late for the juveniles. Bring on the ancient lovers."

Six months later her friend Louise had died, and Charlotte was full of enthusiasm about the funeral. "It was fabulous, darling. But can you imagine which friend said, 'How can you have a viewing in the chapel? That's so barbaric!' Rubbish. Louise would have loved it. She's dead and looked magnificent.

"The makeup people did her eyes—lavender shadow with lots of mascara. And her lips—well, not much you can do about the mouth, but her lipstick was perfect. And William chose a lovely dress of lavender silk. And nobody came. Just William and me, the maid, and some workmen around the house. That was it. I think people are afraid to look death in the face, but Louise looked gorgeous."

A year later all Charlotte's talk was about William. "Everybody tells me he's in love with me. Well, he's still manic, with all that energy released now that Louise is dead. People say I've restored him to his old self. What a relief to be with William. Just a lot of kissing, good food, and wine. I mean it *is* larky. It'll be fun to see who invites me now with William and who wants to get her hands on him for herself."

Events began to take on a rhythm of their own in a sequence directed by Billy Wilder.

"I didn't realize how terrible Louise had been to him. I can't even talk about it without crying. He did everything to appease that woman. I was her best friend, and I didn't see it. He never even took the state law bars when they came back from all those years in Paris. Sure, I'd love to live in his grand house, but first I'd tell him, 'There'll be some changes made today.'

"I told you I can't bear to live alone. My two Big

Fears—coming home to an empty house at night and having no one to pay the bills."

Charlotte married William in the same chapel where they'd said goodbye to Louise. Charlotte made quick work of changing the house, and now with a live-in housekeeper could throw very grand parties to show off her remodeled rooms. But at seventy-five, William was in poor financial as well as bodily health. It became clear they'd have to sell the house and its contents to pay for his medical bills.

"William is not rich. I mean, that was a shock. I was pissed when I found that out and told him so. My dear, we're going to have a tent, right out on the front lawn, with a hot dog stand and a Porto-San, isn't it killing?

"And what a shock to find out that every stick of Louise's furniture, Louis this and Empire that, was *fake*. I was looking forward to at least six figures from Sotheby's. Our security blanket, honey. Well, these two navy-blue suits ran through the house like a dose of salts. They were done in fifty seconds."

Charlotte was torn between delight in catching out Louise and outrage that she herself had been hoodwinked. After their one-day auction with Porto-Sans, they moved to a small house in an ordinary part of town, where William became a full-time invalid.

"Won't do his exercises, won't drink his water, just lies there and makes that terrible wheezing sound—*uuuuumhaha, uuuuuumhaha*—until I turn him over and he stops. I can't eat, I vomit it all up, hypertension. *They*, on the other hand, are eating me out of house and home. That's William and the male nurse who cares for him in exchange for room and board.

"I told William I can't go on this way. He wants to party every week, go dancing every night. 'Dance?!' I squawk. 'You can't even walk.' 'Oh, we'll just dance in a corner, double slow.' I'm terrified he'll roll into a fetus and stay that way—for years. When his lips turn blue, I pray that this time he'll go in his sleep. Every day I pray.

"I keep remembering that moment when we'd both left our husbands and were sitting on the stairs of your house in Princeton and you said, 'What did we do that was so bad that we're sitting here like this?' Sometimes I wish I were old and out of it."

"But we *are* old and we *are* out of it," I want to say but don't, because she's on her own track and not interruptible.

"Please tell me, why is fucking so sad? Was it always this way? Did I feel so sad when I was young and wanted a lot of it, did a lot of it? It's over before it begins. Is that why it's sad? Like a really wonderful meal, all that work, all that preparation, and it's consumed in a trice with nothing to show? Is that what fucking is? A wonderful meal with nothing to show?"

When William did die, Charlotte, at age eighty, quickly married her first boyfriend, James, whom she'd met when he was a naval student at Princeton during World War II and she was in high school. They'd fallen in love dancing cheek to cheek and then went their separate ways.

Sixty years later, boyfriend James, now a father and a widower who'd spent his life in Texas, looked for and found Charlotte on the internet. They married immediately and moved to Texas, summering in Vermont until James could no longer drive and consented to move into a retirement home in Princeton. He died four years later.

When I last talked to Charlotte, she'd had to give up driving and had a full-time nurse in the same retirement home. She gave me scrumptious details about the old folk—the bitches and assholes around her—and then her young male caretaker, who was "divine, darling, and if only I weren't ninety-three . . ." She died a couple of weeks later, but, then, actors never really die.

DAVE

Remember, the filling in our pie needs plenty of flavoring, like garlic and onions, condiments as elemental as the physicality of sex. Fortunately, I really enjoyed the connection of bodies. You met Dave in my first memoir, where I unloaded my guilt about our long affair as friendly married couples in Princeton. We were such close friends, in fact, that we spent many summers together in their villa on the Italian coast. As California hicks, my husband and I reveled in la vie Mediterranean that Dave and Vittoria were both born into and loved to share.

But in Princeton, Dave and I had not been bed pals for two decades before I split from Paul. In our small social circle, we had taken great care to keep our secret secret. In New York, however, Dave was exactly the kind of guy pal I could call upon for advice in my new dilemma.

In New York my adolescent insecurities resurfaced like zits. On streets crowded with half-naked gals flashing Technicolor eyes and ten-inch heels, I felt dowdy and colorless. While my ex-husband was slimming down on Lean Cuisine, I loaded up on Max Factor and L'Oréal.

At fifty-five I was far too old for this meat market, too tough to be roasted or broiled, fit only for the stockpot. But what was the recipe? What kind of soup was this new generation preparing for dinner tables where men talked about babies and cooking while women talked about hedge funds and courtrooms? Women's lib had upset all the stockpots of our social contracts.

So I was delighted to run into Dave unexpectedly, at a reception after a public poetry reading in New York. I spotted him just as a woman with neon-red lipstick passed by and greeted him with "Boring, boring, boring . . . There's not a single man here I want to fuck."

"Who's that?" I asked him.

"A hot-shot poet at nineteen two decades ago," he said. "She gave it all up to become the mistress of the head of the Communist Party in Italy for the past twenty years. Now that they've split, here she is brandishing come-ons and complaints."

Whoa, did I look like that, I wondered, batting mascaraed eyes above lipstick twenty years out of date? And she was only in her forties.

Naturally, Dave came home with me to have a brandy, and we talked and drank and laughed far into the night. We each took a can of beer to bed and continued talking in the dark. The feel of his skin, smooth and silky, hadn't changed, nor the thickness of his neck, nor the comfort of his belly.

"So odd and comforting to have you here," I said.

"I *like* you fatter," he replied.

"My God, I've gained twenty pounds."

"Probably good for you, certainly good for me."

Part of the first generation to take Freud as gospel, Dave believed sex was basically the same for women as for men, but women had to pretend otherwise. We argued about porn, lust, body parts. Boys' puberty, I insisted, was about wet sheets from ejaculation, girls' was about bloody sheets from an inside job. Woman's sex was a hidden chamber designed to hold on to something, man's an erector set designed to hit and run.

I told Dave that I'd confessed my affair to Paul when we broke up. He said he'd long ago confessed all his affairs to Vittoria after she'd caught him in bed with a girl. Vittoria was astonished to learn that throughout their marriage he'd led a double life, in Italy, Princeton, New York.

Dave said of his wife, "I think the Italian in her must have felt 'I didn't think the old fart had it in him.' I'm sure the American in her must have felt totally betrayed. Life had let her down once again, since nobody was ever as pure as her image of them."

To me, she'd remained a naive little girl all her life, which was one of the qualities Dave loved her for. The young girl she'd caught him with I had met once and dubbed the Cow-Eyed Athena since she was so tall and so dumb. But I was biased.

As we lay in bed, we talked about the current rules of the social-sexual contracts that shaped our lives.

"If a guy takes out me out to dinner, the theater, anything in New York, what do I owe him?" I ask.

"Not a thing," Dave replied.

But I knew that was not true. There was always an unspoken barter system at play, yet which was the *pro* and which the *quid*? If I went on a date and paid for everything, would the man *expect* me to insist on screwing him whether he wanted to or not? If I touched him, would he accuse me of date rape?

Dave had his own rules. He complained of his Cow-Eyed Athena, "She comes to me and seems to think I owe her something from ten years ago, now that she's living with a guy her own age who has no money. She wants to use my car when Vittoria and I go to Italy for the summer, but I can't do that. Half of it belongs to my wife. It's time that girl got married. She's not getting any younger."

When we woke late in the morning, clouds were blowing across my skylight with seagulls passing higher up. Mediterranean memories. We made love the way we had so many years before. Sun from the skylight lit up my moon birds, three small ones

of painted wood, which I'd hung from the heavy
beams that held up my ceiling. They seemed to be
caught mid-flight. It was time to get up. Make the
bed. Make a cappuccino. Open the door. Move on.

OLD MAN LEAR

I'd known Eric slightly from parties in Princeton, when I was still married and he a widower with a country estate in posh Hunterdon County and long-standing connections to the arts scene in New York. Once I'd separated and begun to hunt for my own apartment in the city, Eric began to woo me with tickets to Broadway or the New York City Ballet, where he'd been a lifelong patron.

Or to dinners at The Four Seasons with Philip Johnson, Jasper Johns, and other denizens of The Grill or The Pool. "I want a gin martini, straight up with a twist, aching cold and powder dry," he'd command the bartender. Fresh from the suburbs, I was giddy to be let into the inner sanctums of martinis in Manhattan.

To my daughter, who was working at her first job

in New York, I was wasting time and energy on a man nearly twenty years older than me. "Why are you going out with such an old man?" she asked straight out. "Why not someone *your* age?"

"A man my age is looking for a gal your age," I told her. What I didn't tell her was that I was blown away by someone who called me several times a day to say he loved me—*madly*. In my apartment Eric would grab and kiss me before the door was shut, then fall to his knees and tell me he *adored* me. In bed he'd cover me with kisses before I'd got my socks off. For an old man with a white goatee, he was tall, strong, and very commanding. He literally swept me off my feet.

At this time my daughter was dating a man ten years her junior, whom she found to be stupidly childish. We joked that while she was robbing the cradle and I the grave, both men wanted the same thing: to be mothered and mistressed at the same time. What we as women wanted was far less clear to either of us.

Once I'd found my church attic on Thirteenth Street, Eric insisted on physically lugging upstairs my multiple cartons of books and other valuables from my latest sublet to my new home. He equally insisted on helping me make it a home by bestowing on me a potted cactus here, a pair of genuine Picasso plates there, a little enamel teakettle I still use in Santa Barbara every day.

All Eric had ever wanted, he'd repeat like Ferdinand to Miranda in *The Tempest*, was "to serve." For testimony, he mailed me his ten-page vita to prove lifetime service on the boards of the multiple organizations of township, city, county, and state that ran the kingdom of New Jersey.

"Were you disgusted?" he'd asked me.

"No. Why should I have been?"

"You must think the man who did all that must be off his nut." Pause. "Were you impressed?"

"No. Why should I have been?"

"Whatever committee I was on, I seemed to end up as president. Ridiculous."

It took me a while to parse this dialectic, but I began to understand as his story unfolded. He was born in 1907 on a small dairy farm in Wisconsin. In the twenties, his much older brother had become a famous writer, and since he was gay fled to Paris with his partner, a prominent visual artist, to escape the cow patties and morals of the Midwest.

In Paris, the pair were rescued from poverty by a rich American heiress, Janet, who wanted cultural status and got it by setting up a ménage à trois in a villa at Rambouillet. Here the trio played their own version of Noël Coward's *Design for Living* by designing limited editions of books that were themselves objets d'art, with Jan van Krimpen 12-point Romanée typeface, printed on Pannekoek white pre-rag paper. That sort of thing.

By the end of the thirties, when it was time to get out of Europe, they knew one thing had to change: leaving bohemia for the States. Janet would need a front man. "I'll send for my brother," said the writer. Eric came to New York City straight from the farm, a tall, gangling Swede of nineteen with flat-lidded eyes and huge cow-milking hands. They called him "Stud."

"I had absolutely no ambition," Eric told me. "They gave me an uptown mistress and a downtown mistress. And then the whole queer world, but that didn't go. A famous gay photographer tried to seduce me, but when I said, 'I think I'll be moving on,' everyone breathed a sigh of relief. They knew I didn't belong."

For weekend escape from the city, Janet bought a farmhouse restored by Paul Whiteman and surrounded it with stone cottages on a hundred acres in Western Jersey by the Delaware. A studio for each of her artists and a full-fledged dairy farm for Stud. Here Eric could serve others by experimenting with artificial insemination, building a county hospital, and reforming the state prison system, while Janet built her collection of modern paintings.

Janet's story was equally American. She was the granddaughter of a robber baron of the West who built his fortune from railroads and banks at the turn of the century and left a multitude of heirs from eight separate wives. As the eldest grandchild, Janet had inherited the most gold, along with the lawsuits and neuroses of the very rich.

She couldn't stand to have cut flowers or potted plants in her house because she couldn't bear to see them die, Eric told me. No pets for the same reason. No children either, but she insisted on having a child "to feel complete." So after birthing one, she had a breakdown, went to live in a clinic, died there, and left her fortune to Eric to manage. From then on, Eric said, both his brother and his brother's lover seethed with envy, his daughter was estranged, but his duty was to run the place as Janet had commanded.

Eric was my first and last barnyard wooer. He'd had dozens of mistresses over his lifetime but had now suddenly picked me to be his wife at the family compound. Until I set foot in his barn, I'd been puzzled by his self-declared adoration of all women, whether ballet dancers or cows. "Anything with udders," he used to say. Now I saw his face flush with happiness as he introduced me to his black-and-white Guernseys: "Rosie, Gertrude, Melanie."

The barnyard was the only place in the compound free of Janet's ghost. Dinner that night was served in the formal dining room, with Eric's brother and lover. They glowered at me, the newest digger for the family gold. But Emelia the cook, whom Eric had rescued from prison on a homicide charge, took a fancy to me and whispered, "He wants to marry you, you know." I looked up to see a large oil portrait of Janet, unsmiling, above the mantelpiece.

I longed to flee to New York, but I was stuck for the night in a guest room down the hall from Eric's master bedroom. I soon heard the pitter-patter of slippered feet. "Oh, baby, baby, baby," Eric crooned as he threw off his dressing gown and leapt like a mountain goat onto the bed and me. But powder-dry martinis had done their work, along with blood thinners and earlier prostate cancer. His doctor had told him that if he wanted blood where it was needed, cut out the alcohol and soak in a hot tub. His response? "I will never give up the martini."

Eric was working as hard at learning how to woo as I was at learning how to write. Persistence paid off for us, since I was now getting travel assignments as a journalist and needed a strong companion to lug luggage and help drive multiple rented cars.

For a couple of years he was my steady guy, free to travel with me on my hunt for food stories in Wisconsin, New Mexico, Florida, St. Martin's—on assignment. He survived my driving in the desert like a bat out of hell, and I survived his endless rants at tailgaters on narrow mountain roads. Always the nightly martini ritual ended the day when we hit hotel or motel. I'd told him I'd never marry him but loved him as a companion who'd touched my heart.

Each time we returned from a trip, however, to our separate lives in Manhattan and Western Jersey, the green-eyed monster took over. He'd call me several times a day *and* night, certain I was betraying him at that moment with a lover in my bed. Between calls, he wrote letters steaming with love and jealousy.

I knew it was a mistake to say yes to a benefit dance for the New York City Ballet at the Guggenheim, but I thought maybe I could tell him we must part for good. Or maybe I just wanted to go to a party where we would jitterbug as we'd done across the country, he throwing me out with his left hand while pretending to shoot a pistol at me with his right.

I'd been firm that he could not stay overnight with me in my apartment. He delivered me to my door and asked to come in for a glass of water before driving back to Jersey. The moment I shut the door, he grasped my neck with both hands, a farmer's giant hands with prehensile nails so thick he cut them with kitchen shears.

I went limp. He'd often burst into a rage but had done nothing physically violent. Suddenly, I understood why men rape. Rape is less an expression of macho power than of revenge for loss of it. By physical force, a man could command a woman's flesh but not her desire. "I will *make* her want me," his hands said to my throat. "I will make her want *me*."

When I reached up, I could feel the hairs on the back of hands "tough as gutta-percha," as his granny said. Even as I struggled for breath, I felt a twinge of tenderness for this big Swede, who saw it in my eyes and loosened his grip.

"I'll never be on a board again," he said. "I'm too old." His right arm twitched. I'd always seen him as a Lear who'd lost his kingdom and his daughters and had ever poorly known himself. He would never believe that I might love him for himself, not for his money or power, the golden handcuffs of his dependency. What bound me to him were the quirks and oddities that made him *him*. That pink striped shirt he wore with a navy suit, the white hairs of his goatee, the quotes from his hillbilly grandma. "He don't have a pot to piss in or a window to throw it out of."

I was bound by his stories, like his son-in-law who'd raised tigers in cages on the farm to sell to circuses but who went bankrupt, stole some of Janet's paintings, and tried to burn the house down before he fled the country. When Interpol called Eric with a lead, Eric replied, "For God's sake, don't find him. Let him go."

After our Othello moment, Eric finally let *me* go, and to my sorrow I never saw him again. His nurse called me from time to time as his health deteriorated until he took to his bed at the farm, alone after the death of everyone who'd lived there, except for a couple of grandchildren who'd long ago fled to foreign parts. I promised to get down to see him after Christmas, but he died on Christmas Eve 1990, at age ninety.

I don't know why my Eric decade felt so Shakespearean, unless I had to make it so to understand what was happening to him or to me. He certainly opened my eyes to the complexities of Bed Friends, and to the way our conflicts mirrored the self-defining rubric of that robber baron of the West whose daughter he'd wed: "My determination was not to allow anything to stand in my way when I made up my mind."

PATCHMAN

"*When I was* thirty-five, it was a very good year." Actually I was sixty-three and Patchman seventy-two when we began our ritual Saturday Night Date at Broadway Joe's and ended it at my New York apartment listening to *The Voice* transmitted on the radio by Sydney Franklin. On our way to bed, with the smoky sounds of Sinatra in our ears, I blew out the candles as Sydney bade his listeners goodnight. "And goodnight to you, Frankie, wherever you are."

It was a fine romance that caught us both by surprise, Patchman and me, and lasted a decade before our last goodnight. I was in luck when I met Matthew Joseph Culligan in the 1990s. He was a man of many parts and names—MJ, Joe, Mattie Joe—and he was a man who truly loved women.

Born and bred in Washington Heights, coddled

on the bosoms of his widowed mother and aunts, he worked hard from boyhood on with tireless Irish energy. He needed energy to raise three daughters and a son after his wife ran off with the carpenter who'd worked on their family mansion in the fifties, after Mattie Joe had made it big in the media world. I called him Patchman because he'd lost his left eye as a company commander in the Rangers, during the Battle of the Bulge in World War II. He covered the socket with a black patch Scotch-taped to his forehead, and he wore it with the panache of the Hathaway Shirt Man. His remaining bright blue eye twinkled with the cockiness of Jimmy Cagney.

He was used to hardship and loss. The First World War killed his father in the trenches, the Second his brother in Special Forces in the Alps. Nothing, however, dimmed his Cheshire Cat grin. To this day I honor him on my bathroom mirror with a small cutout of that cat, on which I've pasted a black patch.

He was my Irish con man, born with the gift of gab of a County Kerry man who'd traveled the world—his way. On a USIS mission in Thailand for President Johnson, Mattie Joe was given the usual perk of a local girl for his week in Bangkok. Later, he wrote a memoir using the name she'd given him when he said farewell. "I could have loved you, Round-Eye," she'd said. He especially loved her use of *eye* in the singular.

Norman Rockwell had captured that eye in his

portrait of MJ in his prime. "That's the way I see myself," he'd say of the painting, done in the 1960s when he was King of the Hill, appearing in photos with famous people like the astronaut John Glenn or President John Kennedy. On my bedroom wall I've a photo of Mattie Joe on a sofa chatting with President Jack in his rocking chair in the Oval Office.

Not unlike Kennedy, Irish-Catholic Culligan had shot up like a rocket through layers of Protestant Establishment in boom times after the war. The sky was the limit for a guy like Joe, a supersalesman who made the most outrageous lies believable. He sold advertising first for women's magazines, then for broadcasting companies as they morphed from radio to TV. He ultimately became president and CEO of Curtis Publishing Company, whose *Saturday Evening Post* covers had helped create Norman Rockwell's mythical America.

Weekdays he commuted by helicopter from his country estate in Rye to his Philadelphia headquarters, kept a suite at the Regency Hotel in Manhattan, and made *The New York Times*' annual list of the Ten Best-Dressed Men in America.

His rocket was bound to crash, and after internal feuds in the company produced a lawsuit and accusations of mismanagement, Mattie Joe was forced to resign. He tells that story his way in *The Curtis-Culligan Story*, one of his seventeen books.

A golden parachute softened the crash and allowed him to buy a newspaper in Connecticut that soon went bankrupt and landed him on a ledge of rock in Cape Sagres, at the tip of Portugal. He spent a week there imagining himself as Henry the Navigator setting sail for the unknown, while the real Mattie Joe decided whether or not to leap off the cliff.

He leapt instead into a dozen reinventions of himself. "I wrote over a dozen books," he said, tossing them into my lap when we first met in a grand office he pretended was his own. All his books aimed to sell by the arts of persuasion his polyglot inventions.

He persuaded a rich Japanese friend to start up a central database to solve global environmental problems, a smart young girl to start a mood-ring biz that actually did make her a millionaire, his dentist to start a collapsible toothbrush biz, his psychiatrist to collaborate on a book about biofeedback and stress management.

Until his last breath, he tried to persuade one and all of his invention Relatus: a multiuse pipeline across America, layering gas and steam on top, compost on the bottom, fiber optics on the side. He scribbled drawings of his pipeline on every available surface—paper napkins, tablecloths, newspapers, bills—signing them all "Joe Culligan, Inventor."

He persuaded me to collaborate on a movie script about the Galloping Hogan of Ireland's seventeenth century, with his outlawed army of rapparees. So we went to Ireland, where he introduced me to his cousin, Brigadier General Hogan, to reenact and celebrate, pub by pub, the three-hundredth anniversary of Michael Hogan's midnight ride to blow up the English artillery at Ballyneety.

Who would not fall in love with Irish Celtic names like these? Both a Culligan and a Hogan, Patchman was related to all Southern Irish west of Cork. Both a Harper and a Kennedy, I was not, alas, a Celt but a Pict from the wrong side of the British Islands.

Ireland became my Heart Country, during our many visits there, for the unending drama of sun and clouds thundering to grief on rocks and surf. That's why I rented from an American poet friend the shepherd's cottage he'd bought in Coumeenoole, on the Dingle Peninsula. It was the best summer of my life.

Our routine was as fixed as our New York Saturday Night Date. After the big Irish breakfast, we separated. MJ stoked the peat fire, then sat in the sun outside to read Trollope or walk along the beach. I returned to the bedroom loft to string words together for my first memoir, until time for Pub Break. From noon on, Murphy's Pub in Ballyferriter was jammed with Irish voices fueled by Guinness foaming into Gaelic song and dance.

We ate grilled crab sandwiches, read *The Irish Times*, and drove home through hills of wild valerian and purple loosestrife to nap. We woke to tea, then read or wrote until dinnertime, when Sean the neighboring crofter might drop by with an armful of rhubarb to join us in a whiskey in front of the fire.

Later I'd make Sean a pie from the rhubarb, and he'd give me red-skinned potatoes for a shared fish chowder—everything tasting of Irish sea and black earth and green pastures while his sheep nibbled outside our kitchen window and the radio played "million-dollar hits from the forties" like "Stardust" and "Sunrise Serenade."

Patchman fantasized selling his Rockwell portrait and buying an Irish cottage where we'd live the simple lives of artists, although we both knew we were not into marriage or permanent pastoral. Back in New York, it was painful to watch time erode Patchman's body, senses, mind until rituals were all that was left. I'd meet him at one of his clubs, where he'd spend the day telling the same stories, scribbling the same pipeline drawings, cadging extra hors d'oeuvres from his bartender pals.

Only now there were spots on his ties, missing buttons on his shirts. Many of the jackets he insisted on giving me were taped on the inside to hold up linings that had split. He gave me worn-out jackets out of his endless need to give something, and of course I wear them to this day.

His friends trembled for him after a couple of ministrokes left him hobbling on his cane into intersections where he could neither see the lights change nor hear the taxis' horns. Of course, he denied any failing health. "Serve it up to the Lord," he'd say, quoting his mother, while he bragged about his hour of shadowboxing each morning and golf-swing practicing each afternoon.

Gradually, we let each other go. His three daughters, who'd all moved to California, would try in vain to persuade him to leave his beloved city and join them in the West. Instead, he persuaded an old girlfriend to take care of him in his decaying apartment on the Upper East Side.

He yielded to moving west only after a disabling stroke left him speechless. At eighty-three he died sitting up in a chair looking out toward the Pacific, a world away from the crescent of Coumeenoole along the peninsula of Dunmore Head, which stretches its giant green foot into the Atlantic. He was a half world away from the Dingle but still pointed toward sunsets in the West. I miss you, Mattie Joe.

LION KING

For *decades I'd* explored the world's body with a certain detachment as a geographic, culinary, and literary tourist. But in the last decade of the twentieth century, this tourist got swallowed whole on my own turf by my last lover, and my first to be decades younger than me. Instead of me playing Cougar, he sat and yawned as Lion King.

As MJ departed to the West, MB arrived from the East. The Middle East. *MB* stood for Mustafa Burakgazi, whose last name in Turkish means "warrior." He came from one of those ancient ruling families that traced their heritage back to the Ottoman Empire, linking East to West in seven centuries of tumultuous war.

He boasted that when a Western girl had an affair with a Turkish man she was spoiled forever, for "Turks are emotional, passionate, sensual." He added pedantically that Ottoman Turks were not Scythian but Anatolian, as in Suleyman the Magnificent. "Turkic is more correct than Turk."

This Turkic had been a guerrilla warrior in the underground in his teens and an activist journalist in his twenties; he'd been blacklisted with his family after the 1980 coup, exiled to Paris and then New York, where he finally became a history professor. While he claimed to be a rebellious political Marxist, his tribal DNA made him an autocratic warrior and a poet of heroic romance.

Listening to his stories, I was Desdemona to his Moor. My exotic Other. Skin the color of ripe olives, black hair thick and dark, mustache and beard flecked with gray, though he was only beginning his forties when I was in my sixties.

I'd met him through a national organization headquartered in New York City that fought against censorship internationally. I often ran into him on the street of my Village apartment near NYU. During one such encounter, it seemed natural to say, "Come on up for soup and salad." I meant just that. But for him, it was a provocative invitation. He asked for a shot of whiskey instead of wine with his pea soup and tomato salad, then turned on my living room radio and asked me to dance.

On my Turkish rug? At one in the afternoon? Well, why not? He cut a rug with American swing, expertly twirling me toward my bedroom until—*splat!*—there I was flat on my back on the bed, exposed beneath the skylight, every freckle, wart, and wrinkle visible to his naked eye.

But he was already on me, his chest, back, and legs covered with fur, kissing every inch of my body, toes to top, until he exploded like the lid of a pressure cooker over too hot a flame. Were all Turkics like this?

He began to recite Turkish poems, explaining that Ottoman poetry was called Divine, since it was at the same time secular and sacred, ascetic and dervish. Like eros and agape in Western medieval literature. That did it. I was a goner.

I'd actually been to Turkey as a tourist, sailing with my family from Greece to Bodrum, site of ancient Halicarnassus, to explore its underwater archaeology and famous mud baths. As I rattled off my other Turkish tourist sites, he was already planning our next date, outlining his work and home schedules.

He was, after all, head of a hundredfold tribe of Turkish exiles in New York related to the Burakgazis, beginning with his wife, who was his cousin, and their combined sisters, brothers, aunts, uncles, nieces, and nephews. His immediate family numbered forty. Which turned out to matter when he saved the sight of my left eye.

This was after a year of his ritual noon arrival once a week at my apartment for soup, salad, and sex. It suited his schedule and mine. Although it violated my rule of No Married Men, his cultural rules were so different that nothing seemed out-of-bounds.

He adopted me into his tribe as a friend, with only the bed part secret. His father, he explained, had openly maintained, during his own marriage to a cousin, a second "unofficial wife." Ottomans were, of course, famous for their harems.

They were also famous for their feasts, and as an adopted member I got invited to tribal gatherings where wine, chai, raki, and whiskey flowed like the Sea of Bosporus to wash down towers of rice, lamb, and fresh herbs, followed by minarets of honeyed sweets. At the end, men and women sprang from their chairs like bursting pomegranates to twist and twirl, hands waving in the air, hips gyrating, voices chanting in unison to zurna and saz. Someone would always take me home to my apartment no matter how inconvenient to them. I felt it was my first experience of what it meant to be *family*.

When my left eye became seriously infected after a cataract removal, it was Lion King to the rescue. One of his tribe was a noted eye doctor at a noted New York hospital, so he took me in a cab to see her. Immediately, she sent for a glaucoma surgeon to perform on the spot an emergency operation. Six hours later, MB, with a couple of other tribal members, took me home to tuck me in and make sure I was okay.

For the next few months, I wore a black patch just like Patchman's, and often wished MJ were still

alive to laugh at a theatrical entrance into one of
our favorite bars. MB was as impervious to my fa-
cial disfigurement as he was to his own lion's hump,
big belly, and furry back. I never did figure out
what Turkic lenses blocked out for him the chronic
bodily disfigurements of my age: deltas of sags and
wrinkles, acres of moles.

All of my feminist pals abhorred his patriarchal
attitude toward women. But I'd met his mother
when she'd visited him once in New York, a tiny
woman in her eighties. She'd danced with Atatürk
in her youth, had seen one nephew executed and
another made head of state. She was as powerful
as she was acute. Looking at the rugs in my apartment, she pronounced, "Turkish, but not our best."
I adored her.

"Sex to you," her son said to me once, "is a matter
of consumption, a consumable."

"And what is it to you?" I asked.

"In Turkish culture, there's no such thing as individuality per se. The individual is always inside a
circle. He can change one circle for another, but he
is never alone. To be alone is not to exist. Sex is a
moment of intensifying individuality, a sense of self
in relation to another."

We would talk like that while lying side by side
on the bed, physically exhausted by lovemaking that
freed us to say anything, everything, without guilt,
fear, or rejection. "I need you," he'd say. "I need you
like a drug, like medicine, whiskey, pot."

After I'd moved to Santa Barbara, I visited Prinkle in her rest home. Her eyes were bright behind her spectacles, but I'm not at all certain she recognized Flossie. No matter. She was so busy with the new collage she was assembling on her bed that she scarcely looked up.

The catalog at a major gallery exhibition of her works gave her the last word: "I have done so many paintings and drawings of the city, yet I keep finding new things and new ways to see it. The light changes, new buildings pop up. The light and shadow, the volumes—there's always something to *see* out there . . . I look and look at them, but I'm not really *seeing* until I paint or draw them."

Eventually, his body would fail him from time to time with increasing age and ailments, but neither his need nor his affection for other people ever failed. "Do I inspire you to write?" he once asked. No man had ever asked to be my muse. At the same time, he'd tell me about the young mini-skirted students he'd make certain sat in the front row, where they'd have plenty of room to cross their legs.

Long before I moved to California, we'd morphed from Bed Pals to Good Pals, which he remains to this day. As long as we live, we'll be in touch. Every time I whiff a cup of Turkish coffee, see a man dancing with raised hands and gyrating hips, hear the whine of Middle Eastern lutes and horns, touch a furry animal. When the sun sets in the West, I think of Patchman. When the moon rises in the East, I think of Lion King.

WE'VE NOW GOT a magnificent broth, fully flavored. That's all there is to it. Spoon the filling into the crust, put the whole thing in the oven, and let it bake at 375 degrees for forty minutes. Till your house smells like this. Till you're licking your chops like you are now. I'll let you taste it soon enough, dear reader, soon enough. But first, I have to finish my story.

THE VOICE

Ah, yes. The afternoon has come. How do I know? How do I tell the difference when the shadow is all I see?

Listen. Shhh. Do you hear that? Are you listening? Silence, at first. And then—the Voice. The Voice comes from the Med Center every day, same time, right at dusk.

"Help. Let me out."

It's a male voice. Low in timbre, high in pitch, gravelly. Intensely loud. A ritual yell, not a scream. Startling, even though it's by now become predictable.

"Help!"

I'm told he's been in the Med Center something like two years. If I heard his name, I don't remember it, because I never knew him. Will never know him.

Only his Voice. I wish the nurses would just close his window or move his room to the south side of the building, where the windows face an oak grove rather than my backyard.

I don't want to hear him crying for help, because I cannot help him. Nor can the nurses. It's like standing on a beach when you hear someone crying for help way out beyond the breakers. There are no lifeguards, no other people at all. Only the one crying for help, a small arm waving on the horizon. You're paralyzed. You can't swim out. You'll drown too.

"Help!" The voice grows fainter now. He's definitely drowning. On land or sea.

I always wonder: Does he say for all of us what we are most afraid to voice ourselves?

Help. Let me out.

Only Coyote can answer.

THE HEAT CAME DOWN

Why does the Voice clang like a haunting bell? I don't know the man who yells, yet every time I hear him I remember a stranger I met at a cocktail party in New York City. As usual, I didn't know anybody there. It never mattered. We shared the City and Art and our love for it all.

Pouring myself a glass of red wine, I was introduced to a painter named Jack. Thinning hair, bony face, strange almond eyes that looked at whatever wasn't in the room.

"May I pour you some wine?" I asked.

"No." He was nervously intense. Fingers fumbling at his jacket, in his pockets, over his face. "I've been drinking white wine, but I'm not supposed to have any."

Several glasses later, Jack was talking fluently about war writers like James Jones, Stephen Crane. "You don't have to experience war to make art out of it, you know." But the intensity of his voice gave him away.

He said he'd volunteered for the Black Watch in the Canadian Army and landed in Dieppe, where he was captured and kept prisoner in the Baltic for the rest of the war. "Doesn't matter," he said, then continued to describe six months of solitary confinement and hallucinations that allowed him to "see the truth" about himself, "without the bullshit."

"After we were liberated, we were given a list of dead and missing and asked if we remembered what happened to anyone we knew on it. So I look at it, me and my buddies, the ones that survived. Everyone was trying to remember the truth. 'Oh yeah, Sergeant Cooper. I'd forgotten to take the grenades. He got killed and I ran back.'"

Jack turned toward me so suddenly he dropped his wineglass. His eyes were fierce. He put a hand on each side of his head, pressing his fingertips together above his hair like the roof of a church. *"And then the heat came down."* He paused, eyes filling with tears. *"The heat came down."*

I wasn't sure what he meant, but I knew he was exploding at this moment, in this memory.

"I'm in AA." He said it out of nowhere, dropped his hands, bent to pick up the fallen glass.

"Why do you tell me this?"

"Because I thought you should know the truth about me." His right hand started nervously flicking at his fly. He was coming apart at the seams. "I go in and out of AA. I don't want anyone to know I'm drinking."

"Okay."

"I want to believe I can change. People say you have to forgive yourself first, then others will. But it doesn't make sense. It's so circular. *How do you will yourself to change?*"

I was surprised by my response. I still think of it, even now.

"Maybe it's not a matter of *will*, but of *grace*."

NOTES BEFORE
DEADLINE

When you've been alive as long as I have, you've known a lot of people who died. Been to a lot of memorials. Had a long time to think about your own, what you'd like it to be like. The death, and the memorial. For me, it's celebration in the face of both. Revelry and dance and laughter. Wickedness and joy. And I don't mean the staging: the cheesy music, the no-black dress code, the only-happy-memories dictum. I mean to walk out of this life with a wink and a grin, no matter how it happens.

I remember my last "celebration" in Princeton, before moving West, a memorial service for my friend Laura. She and her husband were both activists and journalists in Washington, DC, and had moved to Princeton for semiretirement. In the years since I'd moved to New York City, I hadn't heard from her, but she called me up out of the blue and asked if she could come around for a drink.

We drank a little, laughed a lot, and had one of the best girl-to-girl talks I'd ever had before she took the train home and, two weeks later, killed herself.

What was there to celebrate? She had seemed cheery when I saw her, told me she was writing about the hullabaloo between Choicers and Lifers, as she called them. She'd just come from a meeting of Choicers who called themselves NAPPIES, National Association for the Prevention and Postvention of Infant something or other. We were hysterical with laughter.

Laura loved crazy groups with crazy names. Like the crazy group gathered at the Unitarian Church to "celebrate" her passing. A bearded man in jeans led a group of women in turbans, arms entwined, chanting about Love. We were asked to join the circle while her husband, Mitch, lowered the root ball of a holly tree into a hole.

As he poured her ashes into the hole, Mitch said, "I give Laura's ashes to the earth to become part of the cycle to which we all belong."

A woman next to me muttered, "That tree is going to die, you know. It's too close to the chapel."

Her neighbor whispered back, "Can't transplant it now, it'd be like killing her a second time."

"Hush now, Mitch didn't kill her," came a voice from behind.

"Psht, no secret that their marriage wasn't exactly smooth," said the first.

They all fell silent as Mitch spoke again. "We went to a counseling group once," he said. "Each couple was blindfolded, hands tied behind our backs, and thusly handicapped we were supposed to wander around a room and find our mate. I stumbled around and around until I sat down and cried." He looked like he wanted to bury himself in that hole with the tree. "I never found you, Laura," he cried. "I was always in the dark. Please forgive me."

Did Laura find herself in the dark? She didn't believe in tragedy, yet she'd sat at her typewriter waiting for the sleeping pills to take her life, rolled a sheet of paper to tap out her last headline: "Notes Before Deadline," she called it. Five pages of writing until that last, unfinished sentence—"When the panic comes, and the chaos and confusion . . ."

As the turbaned women led Mitch away, the woman beside me started whispering again. "Gets me so mad reading that final piece," she said. "Here she was, moaning about writer's block while typing up a storm. Why end it? Why not just get on with it?"

I surprised myself when I turned to face her. "Maybe she saw no place to go," I said.

"She came unplugged, that's for the sure."

"At least she was plugged into her typewriter. Maybe she just ran out of words. Maybe there was nothing more to say."

Later that day, I remembered once, long ago,

sitting around with a group of friends and Laura, writing out our own epitaphs for fun.

What Laura wrote: *She loved, she lived, she thought, she felt. She wrote.*

Tick tock.

MOTHER NATURE

End of day is prime time for the changing of the wild
guard. Daytime critters have to gather dinner and
scurry into hidey-holes and nests; nighttime critters
wake up to hunt in the shadows.

Just a few nights ago, as I finished a glass of wine
on this very patio, a sudden shriek made me jump,
and all of my furred and feathered friends disap-
peared in a flash. It was a rare sharp-shinned hawk,
swooping white-bellied into the boughs of the cedar.
Her sharp-eyed, sharp-beaked gaze exposed the folly
of labeling nature "Mother." A mother like Medea,
maybe, ruling a kingdom forever at war over food.

There's no matter of will in the wild, and grace
is but an interpretation of beauty lacking in mercy.
Just hunger. The hunters and the hunted.

When I first moved in, I set up a tall wooden

bird feeder at the edge of the patio, ignorant of the long-term rule of the resident squirrels. They leapt to the feeder with ease, devouring the seed before any birds could reach it.

But I was stubborn. Willful. I got online and ordered all manner of anti-squirrel weaponry. Squirrel baffles, squirrel stoppers, water guns, sonic-wave machines. This was war.

And on the other side of the battle lines, Fat Bastard. He was the biggest of the Gang of Four that regularly raided my patio. The smallest, Slim Pickens, was so scrawny his near-hairless tail made him look like a rat. Slim was a wimp, scared off by the slightest hiss, whereas Fat Bastard would climb my screen doors and stare straight at me, as if saying, *Where the hell's my meal?*

After he pulled down the feeder, food and all, I declared War to the Death. He just sat there on his haunches, tiny paws busy stuffing as many seeds as his mouth could hold, belly bulging. "I'll kill you," I said. I swear, his eyes said, *I dare you.*

So I retreated, abandoning the feeder and dividing the patio into their dining room and mine. One tiny act of revenge: I store the seed outside in a metal bin with a latched handle. No matter how hard Fat Bastard tries, he cannot dislodge that handle. His revenge is to clatter on the lid if I haven't spread the seed by 8:00 a.m. sharp.

But when the sharp-shinned hawk lands—or the red-tailed or the Cooper's, or the great horned owl—or when the fox skitters past, then Fat Bastard retreats. Nowhere to be seen. How he hides with all that girth, I'll never know. But he's invisible until the invaders depart, and then, within seconds, he's back with the rest of the lot to peck and chew and scavenge. No days off. No holidays.

What explains this tedious struggle? There's no epic grandeur here, no Darwinian battle red in tooth and claw. Just ordinary, everyday hunger, enlivened occasionally by something sharper. What am I to make of this endless soap opera on my patio? Am I the only critter on this patio that knows the struggle is in vain? And if the others don't know it, why not?

Where's the grace? What kind of force would dream up such malicious competition? Why can't Fat Bastard, the hawk, Coyote, myself—why can't we be full, sated, finished with hunger?

If death is to bring an inevitable end to each and every player, what does it say about Mother Nature, about our little planet Earth? And what about the sun, moon, stars, Milky Way? When all we can see, with or without telescopes, is to be swallowed by the Black Hole, will we fight on inside the cosmic stomach?

I've grown tired of asking, but the truth about myself is, I never tire of watching. And you, dear reader, are here now, watching with me. I can see that gold flash in your eyes. Must be the sun setting low, that golden hour. Not night, not quite yet, but soon. And don't you think it's time for a little something tasty while we watch?

SMILEY COYOTE
COCKTAIL

Nighttime means a good drink. The sign at my entry promises *Badass Betty's Dive Bar,* and on this, my last night, I want something extra sassy. I know, it's getting late, and you probably have somewhere to be. But have a drink first. I insist. You won't regret it.

Smiley Coyote was a creation of my young pal Meryl in New York. It's a Betty Fussell Biography in Booze: bourbon (for whiskey made from corn); orange juice (for Riverside, home of the navel orange); Campari (for my European travels); Aperol, plus Angostura bitters (for my love of New Orleans); and chili pepper (for my love of Mexico). That said, I play with the recipe all the time, and so should you. Making it up is half the fun. Drinking it is the other half.

INGREDIENTS
1 ½ ounces bourbon
1 ounce Campari
½ ounce Aperol
½ ounce fresh-squeezed
    orange juice
Dash of Angostura bitters
Chili pepper slice, for garnish
Slice of fresh lime, for garnish
Chili powder with salt, for rim

INSTRUCTIONS
Stir everything together and adjust the
pleasure and pain of sweet, sour, bitter,
spicy, and boozy, according to taste—
your taste. Chill in the fridge along with
the serving glass. When ready to serve,
moisten the rim of the chilled glass with
lime juice and dip it into the salt and
ground chili pepper. Serves one person,
if you're thirsty like me.

But you're lucky. Since I know Coyote's thirsty
too, I made a whole pitcher tonight. More than
enough for us all. I like to add a few ice cubes to
mine to lessen the jolt. After all, nothing in my life
is straight up anymore, including my spine. My own
personal advice is to drink a glass of Smiley Coyote
before you even cut into the Coyote Pie. Let loose

the wild child within before you eat. There's no reason to hold back, not tonight.

Now let us raise a glass to Old Man Coyote. He's close, now. So close. And he's starving.

EYE OPENERS

Do you have your glass? Raise it!

My toast is to hunger. Hunger is life, shared life with the wild and the tame. Being hungry is being alive and knowing it, just knowing it. It is the best kind of celebration.

Flashback: I am in New York City at the top of the ninety-first floor at Rockefeller Center. We are celebrating the publication of my first book, *Mabel: Hollywood's First I-Don't-Care Girl*. Since this was my first-ever book party, I'd no idea it would also be my last. Not my last book, but my last Grand Party, the party of my dreams, staged by my editor at Ticknor and Fields, the last of a New England breed of literary publishers. They were under the delusion they had a bestseller on their hands.

So my endearingly Victorian editor invited old

friends of his to the party. Entertainment kings like Sonny Lister, who tap-danced to a live jazz band and led us onto the dance floor to do the Charleston. Here my editor staged a slapstick scene in which, on cue, I threw a custard pie at him while he ducked to let the actor behind him receive it full-face. Both men naively trusted my throwing arm.

Around the room were giant blowups of Mabel's dimpled smile. Tables were decorated with paper fans printed with the rubric *Mabel's Fans*. At the table of honor, my "date" for the evening, the man who escorted me past the many Princeton pals I'd been allowed to invite, was former mayor John Lindsay. He was tall, handsome, and doubtless wondering who the hell Mabel was, let alone her biographer.

He took me up in a private elevator that opened onto a rooftop terrace. When I looked out across the starlit sky of the city turned upside down below me, I knew I'd not died and gone to heaven only because my feet were killing me in teetering shoes, and I had to put my specs on to see what heaven looked like. But there it was, New York, New York, a giant printout of lights pierced by the tiara of the Chrysler Building and the needle of the Empire State. We were on equal footing, the Chrysler, the Empire, and me.

When we looked at the view together, the mayor and me, I asked him, "Did you ever feel like 'It's mine, all mine'?"

He smiled and said nothing. Maybe it was too

large, too glittering, too extravagant, too unreal to be possessed by anybody. I remembered a Princeton moment when I'd starred in the musical *Gypsy*. I told my director that I was having trouble with that final scene when Gypsy Rose Lee becomes Queen of New York and finally tells off her mother, Mama Rose.

"I don't have anything in my past to draw on," I complained.

"But haven't you ever wanted," he asked, "to triumph over some kind of Mama Rose in just that way?"

So simple, so effective. There on the terrace I could imagine what Gypsy Rose might have felt in her diamonds and furs. I could imagine what Mabel, similarly garbed, might have felt as she rocketed from a Staten Island hick to the Queen of Custard Pies.

Mabel dead at thirty-seven, Gypsy at fifty-nine. I thought of the ancient Egyptians who surrounded their entombed royal dead with ordinary goodies from daily life. Like food and drink, dog collars, jewels, mummified cats. Their *Book of the Dead* imagined afterlife as present life. And isn't that why I'd always surrounded my bed with fetishes that will simply extend my life as me? As much a part of me as toenails, warts, hip bones, rotting teeth? We grew up and now grow old together. While flesh goes fast, bone remains. Teeth tell. Even toothless, though, I chew memories.

YOU CAN GO
HOME AGAIN

I was ending where I began, California, but this time not inland Riverside. This time the one place where mountains meet the sea in a strip of palm-lined sand so narrow it can't be ruined the way Riverside was after the war. Santa Barbara means sun without the desert heat of the West or the swamp heat of the East. It was made for oldies like me. Except for the pollen. I had forgotten that paradise also means sniffling and sneezing.

I became so adjusted to my new seacoast environment that it was a shock to return to my birthplace for the sixty-ninth reunion of my high school class of 1944 at Riverside Polytechnic High. I stayed at the fantasy castle of my childhood, the historic Mission Inn, which like me had been rescued from annihilation.

A classmate friend drove me to our old elementary school on Brockton Avenue, just a block from my childhood home. Grant School was swallowed now by the mass of large, low utilitarian buildings of Riverside Hospital that took over the Osteopathic Community Hospital where I was born. The little square box of a house that was ours at 4224 Brockton looked abandoned and forlorn at the edge of a giant construction pit.

On my box, paint was peeling. No porch swing. No flowers. No pepper trees. No small black sign advertising *Elizabeth Harper, D.O.* No car in the driveway. I peeked through the glass window of the front door and rang the bell. Nobody home. I ran around to the back dirt lot where we played cowboys and Indians. They'd put in a hedge and, imagine, a green square of lawn.

The little house next door was dressed up for Halloween with simulated spider webs, ghosts, a dangling body with a severed leg. Made me think of my skinned legs from roller-skating downhill on our block and stumbling into bushes at the bottom to avoid zooming over the curb.

Our reunion lunch was a parody of itself as we gathered at the Spaghetti Factory, which had replaced the old Santa Fe Railroad station.

Twenty-eight of us had made it to a room so noisy that we shouted to each other in vain. The lighting was so dim that even lip-reading was impossible. Although there were plenty of canes, I counted only two walkers and one wheelchair. Most but not all of the women had stopped dyeing their hair. Most but not all of both genders wore hearing aids.

While we listened to a medley of Artie Shaw, Glenn Miller, and other swing favorites of the forties, we chowed down on sandwiches or salads. No wine. Iced tea or Arnold Palmers were favored. I barely recognized our class hero, who had lost everything but his smile. Our class beauty was still glamorous in a red leather jacket with makeup to match.

She reported that at her college reunion at Stanford, Katie Couric had led a panel titled "What Is Happiness?" Our beauty gave us each a sheet of paper, and we had trouble fulfilling our assignment.

As I was leaving, the guy who provided the music sidled up to tell me that he had a crush on me in fourth grade. Golly. I didn't even remember his name. The boy I had a crush on in fourth grade was Frank Taylor, now departed. Frank and I had our first date when his parents took us to the matinee of *Snow White and the Seven Dwarfs*. To this day I remember every dwarf, every scene.

A DANCE WITH TIME

Dancing was the great affair of my life, the movement of the body in time, in music, in rhythm with breath and heart and earth and cosmos. Dance with pleasure, dance with pain. Dance with lovers, dance with death. Shimmy, jiggle, jive. Smile. Always smile. As a kid I begged my parents for dancing lessons, which they couldn't afford. And in any case, dancing was a sin. Fortunately, they didn't forbid movies, so I sat in the dark watching Shirley Temple tapping night after night, toes on the floor tapping with her.

My Shirley Temple dream came true when I moved to New York City and my best friend, Pat, convinced me to sign up together to compete at the Regional Competition of the Fred Astaire Dance Studios at the legendary Copacabana nightclub. There we stood alongside our new friend Annie in the ladies' room. "Dancing has brought magic into my life," Annie said, her seventy-year-old wrinkles hidden in a cloud of ruffles surmounted by a halo of hair sprayed so stiffly she had to use a fork to sculpt it.

There were thirty of us dancers getting ready to compete. This was a first for Pat and me, but Annie was a veteran, the eldest of a group of oldies devoted to our studio teacher, Hernando. Hernando was from Cuba, tall and thin, young and gay, trained in classical ballet but practiced in every dance from waltz to rumba to salsa. His only problem was finding the right Carmen Miranda.

Our problem was finding the dough to pay for our magical transformations. "I've spent thousands every year on private lessons, new costumes, new shoes, facelifts," said Annie as she roughed the soles of her Freed of London spikes to keep them from slipping.

No matter the cost, we all shared the fantasy of defying both age and gravity, becoming weightless, floating and whirling like feathers in the breeze, singing in the rain and dancing in the dark and transcending, if only for a moment, our bodies and lives.

Not that it was that easy. I had to learn, first, to surrender completely to the will of my young teacher. "Let *me* lead," Hernando would snarl. "*Relax*." Only by relaxing would my body melt into his. I was also to suck in my gut, press shoulders down, keep neck tall, stiffen spine, tilt head left, and smile. My body would not obey.

"Don't anticipate the next step. Follow where I put you. *Let your body do the thinking.*"

For the Copa Competition, Hernando decided that my solo dance with him would be an "interpretive" foxtrot to Gershwin's "Our Love Is Here to Stay." I immediately envisioned myself as Ginger in ostrich feathers and sequins, with Hernando at my side as Fred in top hat and tails.

Which is how I, who had never spent more money than necessary on clothes, found myself in the garment district shelling out $500 for twenty yards of sequined peach charmeuse and matching peach lining, $300 for ostrich feathers, $90 for silver shoes, and $200 for a rhinestone choker and earrings.

To put it all together, Pat told me that a divorced woman in her apartment building taught kids tap dancing and sewed tutus for ballet. When I went for my fitting, I entered an apartment littered with netting and feathers, tutus strung on a clothesline over the piano. She assured me she would finish my costume in time.

At my final fitting the morning of the Copa Competition, however, I noticed that my sleeves were different lengths. One too long, one too short. "How can that be?" she asked. I grabbed my dress and feathers and ran. Once home, I discovered that the back zipper was entirely exposed and that only half the feathers had been attached.

No choice but to stitch and glue as best I could and race to the ballroom. Fake palms in neon green surrounded a waxed parquet dance floor slippery as ice. My fear of falling was outdone by my fear of peeing. Annie armed us against both fears. For the first, "Rough up the soles of your shoes, ladies," and for the second, "Don't drink anything. Not even water."

"And *don't* giggle at your fellow sufferers while awaiting your turn." Not even when a bony lady in her eighties stepped onto the floor in a gown sequined with lizards that ran up her arms and neck to her henna-red wig. She bared her teeth at the audience and stared dead ahead while her partner propped her in different positions.

Next came a fat woman so enclosed in pink tulle that she looked like a cloud of waltzing candy floss. After that, a tiny woman no more than four feet tall wearing a column of hair teased so high she looked like a wind-up toy.

At last, it was my turn. Hernando led me to the center of the floor, and I willed my body to think: *I will not tremble. I will keep the line, bend my knees, move with the music, float like a feather, a feather in love.* All went well until the first spin. Timing was off. Had I lost count? I would not panic. *Float like a feather, float like a feather.* Back into Hernando's arms, and a look on his face that said, *Hold it right there, girlie.* Back on track by the time the music ended and applause began.

A night to remember, but nothing like our last

dance in Miami at the National Ballroom Competition. We each got to do a specialty dance with Hernando. Mine was a tango, a commedia dell'arte pantomime that carried us to that second-place trophy sitting on my bookshelf. Then Pat stepped onto the floor dressed as a Biker Babe in a blond wig. The audience roared when Hernando tossed her into the air like a Frisbee and she landed, both feet, blond wig askew.

At the banquet that night, our group toasted one another with bottles of champagne, and I presented Hernando with the Discoverer's Award for his extraordinary achievement of discovering in each of us a hidden dancer. "He made me see it," a wattled oldie said of Hernando. "He gave me an image, and all I had to do was move to flesh it out."

That's what we saw when we looked now at everyone spilling onto the floor to dance—the fat, the thin, the homely, the wimpy, the withered, all of us transformed by spinning the dream of two dancing as one, defying logic, gravity, time, body, death itself. Not, of course, without stashing in our purses a little brush to rough our soles and a fork to comb our hair.

DANCING WITH DEATH

How happy I was to discover that the Casa staged its own form of *A Chorus Line* every four years in our auditorium, with residents in charge of the entire show. Unfortunately, our director, who'd produced the last Casa Follies, had back surgery a month before we were to open this one. As a result, confusion reigned, but no matter. From beginning to end, for audience and performers, our chief interest was in what we wore.

And in our props. Like the American flag. We opened by standing, all who were able to stand, to sing "The Star-Spangled Banner," hands on hearts, voices quavering. While we did not mean to be a caricature of *Waiting for Guffman*, Christopher Guest's sendup of amateur theatrics, it was impossible not to remember it lovingly when a chorus of ten gals took the stage to shout "Another Op'nin', Another Show." Particularly when they were followed by a pair of genuine jitterbuggers, a lawyer in his eighties and a psychiatrist in her nineties.

I was part of the Flapper Five, huddling on the narrow stairs each side of the stage. We have no wings in our auditorium, and the stairs are marked with yellow tape so we don't fall down. We'd rented identical fringed flapper shifts, spangled head-bands, and ostrich feathers. No prob with flapper bobs, since every woman at the Casa wears her hair short, except for me. So I rented a dark-brown wig with bangs and a bob.

"Unacceptable," the choreographer cried. "I don't recognize you."

"You must wear that all the time," countered a fellow dancer. "You look so much better."

I resolved the issue by saying, "I'm not myself. I'm Flapper Flo."

That worked for the Charleston but not for our second number, a line dance to "Singin' in the Rain." For this we had to do a quick costume change by running outside into a storage room to find our raincoats and hats, white pants, and red T-shirts, plus one umbrella each.

Meantime, onstage the Dorinda Twins sang and danced "Side by Side" before twelve Ziegfeld Girls paraded to "A Pretty Girl" in gowns appropriate to their assigned calendric month. July was Auntie

Sam in red, white, and blue. December was a Snow Queen in white fur and mistletoe.

This was the Follies' climax and our Rain Dance the final number. Our dance was far simpler than the Charleston, but there were twice as many of us onstage to fumble opening our pesky umbrellas with arthritic fingers. We performed without mishap but for one umbrella that exploded when opened exactly the way umbrellas do when it's pouring rain on city sidewalks and you've just fallen in love and long to stomp in the nearest puddle.

The fumbler was the hit of the show before the audience rose to sing "God Bless America" while our entire Follies cast filed out to line the corridor from the auditorium to the main building like a giant reception line at Buckingham Palace. The audience ran this gauntlet snail-like in canes, walkers, and wheelchairs, transformed by the magic of theater.

For a moment we had come together in Let's Pretend, a moment where all of us could sing and dance and kick up our heels and fall in and out of love and stand united to serve our country in our tragicomedy before exiting, one by one, from the stage.

HAPPY NEW YEAR

The sun is out. The air is cold and fresh, after a night and day of steady rain. Rain did not dampen last night's New Year's Eve party in the Casa dining room, which began at 5:30 p.m. and was over by 8:00. That's p.m., not a.m. as in days of yore, when the midnight countdown in Times Square was the beginning of festivities, not the end.

I contemplate last night's miracle. The Miracle of the Man Who Doesn't Dance. By definition, few of our male residents rush to the dance floor without heavy prodding from their wives, even men who did learn to eat quiche.

But there was a new couple who'd arrived from the East about a year after I did, and the moment I saw them, so tall and beautiful together, I assumed they were a dancing pair. No. Firmly no. They piloted airplanes together, captained sailboats, but dancing? "We don't dance."

The husband confessed that he had danced when he was courting his wife-to-be. "But I got the girl, so I don't need to dance anymore." Fighting words to a believer in the inherent joys of bodies moving to music, quite apart from courtship rituals.

I was plotting tactics like lighting a match to his shoe for an old-fashioned hot foot, but an older friend beat me to it. This was my ninety-six-year-old pal who a couple of years ago had spent two months in a brace for her right leg after we'd crashed doing a swing dance at the Halloween party. Same band.

And sure enough, with the first notes of the Old Timers' Jazz Band, a group whose combined ages matched our own, my swinger pal jumped to the floor in a shimmy and a shake. I rose to join her, but my table as one yelled "No!" They'd yelled the same to her, but she'd paid no attention. No one tells *her* what to do, she just *does*. And there she was, happy as a spinning clam, all by herself.

To the rescue, the Man Who Doesn't Dance. He's wearing a black tux with a green bow tie to match his cummerbund, and he's dancing. First with my little pal, then with his wife, and finally even with me. My friend's knee is miraculously cured, his wife apparently loves being courted, and I am grinning from ear to ear. Most of all, the dancing man is smiling. He looks *happy*. As do countless others who join us on the floor.

Perhaps the champagne, or the lobster bisque, or the grilled chateaubriand, or the devil's food cake had something to do with the devilish joy of that dance. Or maybe Father Time worked his magic of actually creating a New Year.

EYES & EARS

The more slowly I move, the more time speeds up. Where did it go—last weekend, last year, last decade? Today? Just now, sitting with you on the patio, I could almost see the colors change from Meyer-lemon yellow to navel orange. Quickly, too quickly, it's dark.

Wait. Is that my dinner guest at the door? Is it time? It can't be time. I'm not finished yet. Ah. No, it's just the wind, the breath of the wind knocking at the branches.

It's not just time that goes. It's the body. Senses, functions, looks. Till the body that's yours doesn't feel like your own anymore. Whose hands are these, mottled and bony? Whose face, pale and crease-worn as old paper?

Decay. Most of the oldies I've known fight it, tooth and claw. A war as futile as my war with the squirrels. We are all going to be evicted from these bodies. When and how is the only question. Slow-motion or sudden. I knew long ago I didn't want to fight it. I'd like to dance with it, at least, hungry till the end of our foreplay.

Still. The losses mount. The hardest of which are the eyes and the ears. As darkness falls, outside and in, I think of my childhood. The grandma of my next-door neighbor in Riverside was totally blind and sat by the radio day and night, knitting. My own Grandma Kennedy was bedridden for a couple of decades by glaucoma and arthritis, though this didn't prevent her from commanding each member of the household to execute her wishes from the bed on which she lay, day and night.

Like other schoolkids of the time, I often played blindman's bluff alone in the living room, feeling my way around with eyes closed, bumping into furniture and walls. The national icon of blindness at the time, Helen Keller, had said that the other senses would sharpen, but all that intensified was my sense of fear.

Nowadays all I associate with sight is pain. Since I was diagnosed with glaucoma thirty years ago and an emergency operation, I knew I would one day be totally sightless. The drops and medicines I put in my eyes over the years may have slowed the process, but they also provoked an allergy to eyedrops,

preservatives that sped up the darkness and in-
creased the pain.

Today, I can see shapes, fuzzy outlines, but not
details. It makes recognition of other people prob-
lematic. Is that my dear friend or a total stranger?
Are you the same reader who knocked on my door
this morning, or are you someone else? I greet everyone the same, just in case: "Hello, thank God you're
here." I long ago lost the vital depth dimension to
see stairs, curbs, cracks in the pavement. I hang on
to my walker as I would a guide dog. Day or night,
doesn't matter. Bright lights are, alas, as blinding as
the dark.

I'd hoped what might sharpen in lieu of sight
would be hearing, but my ears are in no better
condition than the rest of me. Oldies of my grand-
parents' generation used ear trumpets, or the home-
made variety of a cupped hand round the ear. No
trumpets today, but conversations comparing the
function, cost, quality, and brand of different hearing aids are as constant as conversations about the
weather in the old folks' home. Most of us know
we're lucky to be able to tuck the wire in the canal,
curl the coil behind the ear, and get by with only a
few misunderstandings.

Still, going deaf feels worse sometimes than going blind, because you lose connection—not just
with other people, but with yourself. My closest
neighbor and breakfast club friend, also named
Betty, was stone deaf, beyond the reach of any aid at

all. Had been for a long time. She'd been skilled at lip reading, but as her vision wore down, we added a school slate and chalk to our breakfast tableware. Even after she moved into personal care, Betty met us weekly to chat, filling our slate with the latest rumors. Both of us Bettys used our walkers as chairs and scribbled furiously on our slates, laughing as we passed them back and forth.

A couple of years before she reached one hundred, Betty's daily mantra was "I want to go to sleep and not wake up." We understood. She was so bright, so alert, no matter how deaf or blind or decrepit. Always the caring nurse she'd been since World War II, pushing her walker around the perimeter of the property and waving at everyone she saw.

I can still almost hear her saying her last words: "Ta-ta, see you on the other side."

HAIR & TEETH

As a child of Victorian parents, not until I began to have babies at age twenty-seven did I experience what it meant to have landed on this earth inside a mammal's flesh and fur. Along with my first baby, I gradually discovered with wonder and awe my own ten fingers and toes, my own upper mouth and the udders that fed her, the organic nature of the uncontrollable liquids that poured from my own lower mouth. I was astonished by the oddity of the whole process, guided first by Dr. Spock and then by *Our Bodies, Ourselves.*

Only now that my baby is in her sixties do I realize I'm traveling backward toward my own babyhood, one faltering step at a time. Like a spoiled child, my body demands constant attention, interrupting my concentration by day, sleep by night. It's taking over, dammit, erasing my memory box, already full of holes and suffering water damage. The body I launched in my maturity as Betty Harper Fussell is in full retreat to adolescent Betty Ellen Harper, who will eventually become Baby Betty.

HAIR

I always wore my hair long, from pigtails to a single braid to a cascade of wavy blond, because it grew too fast to bother cutting. But in my family's house, Saturday was hair-wash day in preparation for Sunday, the Day of Church, Dinner, Nap. Saturdays I washed my hair in the large sink in the basement where we washed our clothes on a washboard. Because my hair was so full of tangles, it always took me a long time to brush it dry in the backyard sun, listening to the Metropolitan Opera broadcast courtesy of Texaco.

Where I live now, long hair worn loose is not fashionable and often frowned upon. But I am too lazy to put it up in a bun and it's too thin to wear bobbed and I'm not going to dye it white just to fit in. Besides, I like the feel of it when a high wind suddenly blows off my Panama hat and my hair swirls in the air wild and free.

TEETH

I'm sure you don't want to hear about the latest root canal on my third molar, upper right jaw. But how many of you have had a root *amputation*? Or even heard of it? Google *RootAmp* and you'll find multi-ple ads for a root-amplifying hair spray but noth-ing about teeth. Teeth are the subject here and will remain so until I stop talking or eating. And that's why I wanted to save the next-to-last molar in my upper right jaw. No molar? No steaks, nuts, apples, tough bread crusts, crisp cookies. Sob.

So I violated my edict "No more root canals." But I was faced with a *no chew* on either side. Intol-erable. My regular dentist sent me to the *endodontist* (root-canal specialist: *endo* means "inside," and *donte* means "tooth." See how simple it is?). This endo-dontist was a cheerful Austrian woman who asked with some frequency, "Does it hurt?" Of course it hurt. I'd warned her I was super-duper sensitive to pain and required two or three times more Novo-cain than most. I would far prefer she use gas, but dentists are phobic about anesthesiologists; they worry that oldies like me will drop dead. As root canal-ers always do, she pooh-poohed my fears with pain-free promises.

The prelude to my ensuing *Eroica*, conducted by the endodontist, was a scuffle with her young assis-tant who tried to insert an entire X-ray machine into my right cheek. But I breathed deeply, as instructed, and didn't throw up. The *allegro con brio* movement began when Dr. Mengele pushed the pain-killing Novocain needle farther and farther into my gum.

A long, silent numbing interval before the *marcia funebre* began with the ritual procession of instruments, percussive sounds and vibrations, as Dr. M. yanked my mouth around and assistant Y. sprayed water in and sucked it out. My left leg jerked up, and Dr. M. told me to raise my hand if I felt any pain. "You can feel this?" she asked in disbelief. My hand shot up as well as my foot. "Hmmmm." She applied some useless unguent.

In good German fashion, Dr. M. had given me my choice of stuffed animals to hold. Evidently, she'd worked on children of all ages. I squeezed my soft brown furry puppy tightly with both hands. What a godsend. Why didn't all dentists do this? Unfortunately, there was nothing to do about my feet, which would kick up automatically when any new instrument attacked my mouth. "Don't worry, it's not *you*," the doctor reassured her assistant. "She can't help it."

An hour and a half later, after the *coda* of crowning and biting, we were done. My temporary crown was composed of a material called gutta-percha. I learned from Google it meant "the latex sap from a Malaysian jungle tree." It's much cheaper than gold. But my molar was guilty of "tooth resorption," an inflammation caused by loss of tooth structure within the root as the result of "prolonged insult." My God. My teeth were alive with the sound of insult. Again, who knew? I always thought of my teeth as extensions of jawbone, far more immortal than flesh—those grinning skulls of Day of the Dead. But I didn't know each tooth bone is filled with a pocket of "dental pulp," those cells, blood vessels, and nerves that feed each root just as they feed bone and flesh top to toe.

"Prolonged insult" required an appointment with my periodontist, the gum doc, to amputate my "third root," whatever that might mean. "Oh, don't worry," said his assistant. "It's nothing at all like a root canal. It's like a manicurist filing and painting your fingernails." I haven't been to a manicurist for half a century and remember it hurt when she pushed back each cuticle.

So it was back to the vomit-inducing X-rays. Back to the painkiller needles and my animal howls. The doc was used to me, but his assistant was new. Back to the drills, flushes, and suck-ups, this time ending with needle and thread. "Dental surgery is not at all like a manicure," I muttered. "Ah, perhaps not," Doc laughed. Perhaps he had a sense of humor. How could anyone be a dentist without one? "It is done," he proclaimed as he tied the last thread with a flourish. My grandmother used to correct me. "Roasted turkeys are *done*; human patients are *finished.*"

Human patients are never finished. Next week's appointment is for the removal of stitches, provided there is no infection. And after that, an appointment with my regular dentist for a permanent crown to add to my Fort Knox collection. Another month of *no chew* to protect the gutta-percha crown.

What I miss most are roasted cashews, popcorn, and steaks. But since it took ninety-some years to grow and maintain this one molar, perhaps I shouldn't complain that it takes a dental village to save it. And maybe I should check out that Root-Amp hair-spray ad with the hope of salvaging a few more hairs as well as teeth.

TAILBONE

Splat. I've banged my tailbone seriously three times in my life. First when I was fourteen, playing tennis on the outdoor courts at Riverside Poly High School against my major opponent. I'd stepped forward to return her serve, swung hard, slipped on the concrete, and fell flat on my back, tailbone first. Above me the bright blue sky looked as it always did, but the number of faces peering down at me did not.

"You need help?"

"I need to get my breath."

Hands reached under my shoulders and lifted. Yikes. Something hurt like hell. That's one way to find out what a tailbone is.

As a lover of slapstick movies, I'd laughed at hundreds of pratfalls in black and white. But now my tennis whites showed a few drops of blood. I was able to walk. Nothing seemed broken. Someone drove me home, and when my osteopathic stepmother examined me in my bed, she found a big bruise on my tailbone and told me my period had begun. All I knew about periods was that most of my friends had them, but they were something you never mentioned unless you wanted to get out of gym.

My second major splat was in Otavalo, Ecuador, when I was fifty-eight on vacation at Hacienda Cusín, owned by an Anglo-American couple, friends of mine in New York. Everyone rode horses at the Hacienda, and since I am not a horsewoman I asked for a gentle mount. A group of us left the Hacienda to ride a few miles through nearby woods, and all went well between my horse and me until I turned him to go back.

Most of my group were far ahead of me when my horse suddenly smelled *Home!* He set off at a gallop while I clung to the saddle horn, crouching to avoid decapitation by low-hanging branches. I'd been told to pull hard on his right rein and turn his head to slow him down. Annoyed, he stopped dead and bucked me over his head. *Splat.*

He galloped on, heading for the chow line, while I lay where I was in the woods. Fortunately, a straggler in our group came along the trail in a few minutes, told me to lie still, and went for help. Helpers came and carried me on an improvised stretcher back to my room. I spent the rest of my stay at the Hacienda with an icepack strapped to my tailbone.

Everyone was sympathetic as I hobbled about the Hacienda with a cane, but I nursed a secret grief. The night of my fall, the owner had promised to take me into town to a dance hall to teach me to salsa. He was a handsome guy, and the Ecuadorian landscape encouraged fantasies of romance. A little night music with the sound of mariachis in the moonlight. Alas, instead of soap opera, I got slapstick.

My third *splat* was at age eighty-eight at Casa Dorinda, during our annual Halloween Dinner with a live jazz band and everyone in costume. Since this was election year, a pal and I hosted our table costumed as Crooked Hillary and Dirty Donald. Amazon had equipped us with realistic face masks and wigs, one orange, one blond. I stuffed a pillow into my white shirt beneath a red tie and dark suit. Our real identities were perfectly secure.

It was a crackerjack party with lots to drink, as a live band of oldies played the swing music we loved of the forties and fifties. There are never a lot of dancers, but those who do take the floor are either couples who've danced together for the last sixty years or solo gals who've always been dancing fools and are not about to stop now.

When my ninety-four-year-old psychiatrist pal beckoned to me from the floor, I couldn't resist. She's as short as I am tall, but we were swinging good to the music in our hearts, our knees, our toes.

The floor was ours as I swung her out on a turn and somehow we both kept going. She fell forward as I fell backward. *Splat.*

I looked up and saw familiar faces—fellow residents, a staff member, a doctor asking questions: "What is your name? What is the date? Where are you?"

"Please, just help me up." Someone's fingers were touching the top of my skull. "Ouch." I felt a goose egg. I didn't need to touch my tailbone to feel the bruise. Many hands raised me into a wheelchair. A nurse wheeled me home with my mask, my wig, and a bag of candy corn. My partner had been wheelchaired to the Med Center with a rebroken ankle. There might be a hairline fracture in my ancient tailbone, but what would it matter? There was nothing for it but weeks of ice packs, pain, and rest. Meantime, I could watch Laurel & Hardy and the Keystone Kops, and Mabel & Fatty & Charlie and all those who'd taught me how to laugh when somebody else went *splat.*

THE BOD

LUNGS

Human time is based on breath: in/out, in/out, one/two, one/two, tick/tock, tick/tock, repeat. The rhythm of music, the rhythm of dance. Human time begins and ends in the Bod, and inside the Bod breath rules. We can alter the rhythm of breathing but not its necessity. We can speed it up or slow it down to alter the brain, which some docs say has the consistency of butter. I like the image of butter-brain more than computer-brain. Both are wired to a binary system, but one is organic and the other robotic.

I learned about breath when I began to do yoga, which is the opposite of robotic exercise. I liked the language of pressure points and energy centers, and I liked learning how to focus on the process of breathing. I liked the action of locating my Bod's Field Energy Center two fingers below belly button in front, just opposite the top of tailbone on the back. I liked imagining a rope at the back of my skull pulling spine straight up to the sky. Shoulders back, chest forward. In fact, all the imagery of yoga connects my little Bod to the big world's big Bod.

I liked meditation connected to action. Tai Chi was paradisal in language and movements like Laughing Man, Painting the Waves, Flying Eagle, Needle at Sea Bottom, Woman Waves the Shuttle, Throwing the Net, Holding the Sun.

What could be better for aging bodies and minds in all their anxieties and fragmentations than focus? Stillness. Listening to my body breathe, slowly in through the nose and out through the mouth. Clearing out brain, skull, connecting them to diaphragm, belly, backbone, tailbone, breathing deeper and slower, aware only of breath and the tiny black spot in the middle of my forehead, changing color from black to white to orange to purple. Oblivious to all but this inner/outer eye suspended in the black hole of the cosmos. Life changing. Death changing. Here. Now.

GUT

In childhood I felt strongly that the Bod was my enemy because it was so frequently out of control or, more accurately, in total control. I speak from the Gut as a full-fledged veteran of the Constipation

Wars, in which my entire family was engaged. Gut was the curse we were born with, our cross to bear, like our dear Lord's, in atonement for our sins. Heavy duty for an organ, with its twenty-four miles of convoluted tubing.

My grandma took an enema every single day, occupying fully the tiny toilet on our back porch. My dad underwent his colonic irrigation every Sunday afternoon in our upstairs bathroom, administered by his D.O. wife. A pure spirit was insufficient without a purified gut. For hours at a time, neither bathroom was available to my brother and me.

Gut was the whispered subject of our daily conversation, but nothing associated with the body could be mentioned out loud. It took me years to learn that my father suffered from "abdominal adhesions" and my grandmother from "intestinal malrotation," which meant her small intestine was on the wrong side. My genetic heritage forced on me a daily tablespoon of cod liver oil each morning before school, and if that didn't do it, a couple of tablespoons of stewed prunes or figs. And if that failed, the dreaded enema.

There were occasional mishaps of the reverse kind. One memory burns. I'm in the third-grade class taught by Mrs. Redwood at Grant School, just down the block from our house. I am writing at my wooden flattop desk attached to its own chair, in which I'm having a lot of pain in my gut. Mrs. Redwood suddenly turns and looks around the room.

"Who made that terrible smell?" she asks at the exact moment I feel a sudden warmth below. No one answers, but all follow their noses and point at me. Teacher comes to my chair, sniffs, jerks me up by the arm, marches me into the girls' room and puts me in a booth. "Stay there," she orders. "I'm calling your grandfather to come get you."

He too is a D.O. with an office nearby. I wait, recognizing the wet stuff as precursor to the real problem, a large turd stuck in the opening it's supposed to come out of. Grandpa arrives with a big bath towel, which he wraps around me to get into his car. In his office, he sits me on a chamber pot and goes to work with rubber-gloved hands. The pain is intense until the extraction is complete. When we get home, he helps me upstairs and tucks me into bed, where I'm too tired to cry.

As I grew older, I learned how to cope on my own with this kind of power play executed by Gut no matter what I ingest to ease his way. Bran, Prunes, Figs, Mineral Oil, Miralax, Dulcolax, Magnesium Citrate, threats of the Clinic and You-Know-What. Gut may be punishing me for an additional hazard I can do nothing about, the massive Piles that increasingly block the exit. Most of the time Gut works entirely on his own, independent, rebellious, quirky, willful. I can't predict his actions, only respond to them. By now, I should enjoy his rogue character, but I don't, because I am wholly in his power. I know I'm not alone in this condition in the old folks' home, but while we talk endlessly about food, we never, ever talk about shit.

Why is something so universally shared by all critterdom taboo only among our two-footed species? Birds do it, bees do it, dogs—well, look at them. They smell one another's poop and assholes freely, with no hesitation or shame. Rather, it's a ritual greeting, like "Hi, how are you?" Maybe this is Gut's revenge on a species whose upper mouth boasts the divinity of Brain and scorns the Brute below.

NAUGHTY BITS

I worry that I can't find on my computer the draft I wrote less than a month ago on the Naughty Bits, as Monty Python used to call them, because I've already forgotten what I filed it under. Like my worry that I can't apply Efudex to the back of my hands for skin cancer because I can't find the tube. Or my worry that something's wrong with my recent waking up in the morning and masturbating because of that old familiar pang in the Naughty Bits. But at ninety-two? What's wrong with me?

Fifty years ago, Bod said loud and clear, "Rub me, rub me fast as you can." My NB were slow to rouse but, once launched, inexhaustible, as I learned over the extended dark ages of my ignorance. During most of my life, for a girl to adventure alone into such territory was as tribally forbidden as a trip alone up the Amazon.

But old age was supposed to diminish appetites,

certainly sexual ones. So why now? I haven't had sexy dreams or body pangs of that sort for the last decade. Bod has been too busy pumping blood through blocked arteries, rushing to defend cuts or bruises against bacterial invaders. So I laughed aloud when Bod woke me up with that lower-mouth pang that says, "Feed me."

I've long wondered at the topology of the humanoid mouth. Like, how come we have but one orifice for both eating and speaking? Which necessitates both an outer pair and two inner pairs of lips? The outer pair opens on teeth, tongue, and tubes that channel food intake one way and air another. Food goes from pharynx to esophagus to stomach. Air from voice box (*larynx*) to windpipe (*trachea*) to lungs. And how does our voice box work? Air passes through the inner pair of lips (*epiglottis*) to vibrate the vocal folds (*glottis*) that open and close over the voice box.

The females of our species are even odder, because we have two mouths, one upper and one lower. Lower mouth (*vulva*) has two pair of lips, outer and inner (major and minor *labia*) to protect another pair of openings: the small one (*urethra*) expels liquid waste, the large one (*vagina*) takes in food (*sperm*) and expels the fertilized egg (*fetus*) when ready. The female Bod's pleasures and pains are thus fully internal and integral to the whole Bod in a way that the male's are not. For females, maybe feeding either mouth is always a sexual act, just as a sexual act is always a form of feeding. Males who fear women as predators with *vagina dentata* may be onto something. As are females who say, "Tell me how a man eats, and I'll tell you how he makes love."

Maybe instead of worrying about why my lower mouth should want pleasuring in old age, I should consider eating an extra scoop of coffee ice cream with chocolate sauce for breakfast in bed. In either case, not to worry.

MEANTIME

How weird it is to live without a future. Now my only tenses are present and past. Now my major struggle is to hold on to the present so I don't slip robotically and remain glued in the past. I know all the danger signs:

"I used to get up at five o'clock every morning and work out at the gym for an hour."

"Where are the cloth napkins? We never had paper napkins for lunch when I was a child."

"Do you know how much they're asking for that bungalow down on Middle Avenue? You wouldn't believe it!"

I try to avoid my unconscious denial of change, denial that everything has changed and will keep on changing *without* me. As Heraclitus told me, I'm as irrelevant to time's eternal current as a pebble rounded in a stream. Why did I think I was better than a pebble? More important? Doesn't a pebble have pebble thoughts in its own language? How would I know if I don't listen to it speak? As the poet says, "Pebbles cannot be tamed / to the end they will look at us / with a calm and very clear eye."

Why don't we get it? After all, we're in this together, on the same lifeboat or raft we've seen in a hundred movies, paddling for a shore that long ago receded into the mist while one by one we slip off into the sea. We paddle for an island we will never reach, ration water for a survival we will not survive. Surely we have something vital to share but are puzzled by what that might be.

For sure it's not based on the tick of time that drove us toward a future. So why do we paddle so mechanically, so anxiously? Let's drop our oars. Let's tell one another stories that defy real time with story time. Stories that make all times reverberate with the intensity of that distant seagull's cry. I'll tell you mine and you tell me yours. And if I slip off midsentence, no matter. You already know the ending.

I'M COMING, GRANDMA

Every Sunday morning I turn on my radio to listen to choral music for two hours on the KUSC classical station.

Lying in bed, eyes closed, I hear the voice of Grandma Harper shooing me out of the house like one of her bantam chickens out of the coop. I am five, dressed in my Sunday best of tight pigtails, ironed cotton dress, and Mary Jane shoes.

"We mustn't be late for Sunday school," Grandma warns.

Grandpa is already in his old Ford V8, warming up the motor.

I hear today's Sunday school reading from the illustrated Bible as our voices respond in song. "Tell me a story of Jesus, I want to know."

Afterward, Grandma takes me to our church pew

for the main service, where I will fidget during the endless sermon after the ritual rise and sit, sit and rise, to the rhythm of Jesus's death and salvation in anthem after anthem.

Whenever I hear liturgical music, I see Grandma, so strong in faith, so frail in body and eventually mind. I see her lying in bed at the California State Rest Home she was condemned to for the last decade of her life while I went off to college and the world. During my final visits, she held my hand tight while she floated down the Mississippi River from Illinois to Nebraska.

"I'm coming," she'd say to her waiting sister, as she also said to her husband and to Jesus. They were already there, waiting to welcome her to heaven. Glory Hallelujah.

Grandma has been waiting for me patiently. Both of her sons have already come. Some of their kids have come too. And theirs. Tears come easily to me especially now, while I talk to my daughter, write to my son, wait to look Coyote in the eye.

I feel him, just behind me. Waiting.

"I'm coming, Grandma. I'm coming."

TIME'S UP

Ah, dear reader. Night is falling quickly now, inside and out. In the twilight, my blind eyes see things strangely. That full moon, its white orb winking at me through the branches of my giant tree. Eyesight being what it is, sometimes I see two moons, even three. Ghost moons, but I can't tell which is which. In my mind, though, I can still see that mysterious calligraphy we translate into a smiling moon face. I pay my respects to her beauty with hand on my heart and gratitude on my lips while she smiles down at me.

But wait a minute, wait a minute. Is that a wink? Is that you, Coyote, is that you up there winking, smiling, beckoning me? Are you even real or a figment of AI?

You must be able to see it, dear reader, and what big eyes you have—tell me, is he here? Is it time?

It must be time. Let me walk you to the door, dear reader. Perhaps Coyote is standing there, waiting to be let in, pawing at the mat. Perhaps I missed the knock on the door. You might have heard it, what with those big ears you have. Tell me, did you hear a knocking?

Here, here, take a slice of pie for the road. Take another drink. Take the recipe too. I can hear the growl of your stomach, hungry still. What an appetite you have. Here, take everything. Take anything you want, anything at all. The books, the pictures, the vases, the clothes, the jewelry, the knives. Every item has a story. Take it all. You can carry it—you seem so strong, so tall, your hands so big.

Now go, dear reader. Be on your way. I have sated your hunger, filled your belly with words, filled your ears with memories, and given you reason to laugh along the way. There is nothing left.

Why are you still standing there? Why are you smiling at me like that?

Yes, I do cherish the gleam of your teeth as you grin. And what sharp teeth they are.

Mm, yes. The better to eat it all up, my dear.

Tick.

Tock.

Tick.

. . .

Acknowledgments

Thanks go to the following . . .

Kelly Grogan, Joan Tapper, Jack Shoemaker, Megan Fishmann.

Rosalind Fussell, Sam Fussell, Alex Retana and family, Dennis and Jefi Harper and family, Norman and Florence Lind and family, Hilary Morgan and Robin Dublin.

Nancy Oster and family, Meryl Rosofsky and family, Eileen and Susan Culligan, Dawn Mobley, Felicia Campbell, Vivian Ramos, Anna and Joey Kallas, Mary Heebner, Macduff Everton, Hanna Foraker, Paul Rankin, Sandy Walcott, Marc Goldman.

Michelle Joanou, Sandy Parkerson, Dr. William Koonce, Gisele and Brian McDermott, Jere and Fima Lifshitz, Kristin Demong and Charles Atkins, Karine Clark and Donald McCall, Bob and Carole

Nicholas, Donna Kelsey, Larry Liddle, Eva and Yoel Haller, Ingrid Hunzer, James and Nancy Taylor, Peter and Linda Beuret, Candace White and John Manson, Tracey Goforth, John Patel, Linda Saunders, Nina Schooler, Penny Arntz, Gina Jannotta, Carolyn Kincaid, Jean Keely, Eric Chavez.

And to the many friends who have gone before me: Charles Weis, Irene Hymanson, Pat Adson, Betty Edwards, Freddy and Margaret Perutz.

Born in Southern California in 1927, **BETTY FUSSELL** grew up in Riverside but lived for most of her life in the New York area. Best known for *The Story of Corn*, she is the author of twelve nonfiction books, ranging from biography to cookbooks, food history, and memoir. Her essays on food, travel, and the arts have appeared in scholarly journals, national magazines, and newspapers, including *The New York Times*, over the past fifty years. A specialist in Shakespeare, she has taught English and American literature and the history of food and its importance to American culture at colleges and universities across the country. She has lectured to audiences everywhere from the Metropolitan Museum of Art to the Iowa State Fair. Her many awards include the International Association of Culinary Professionals' Jane Grigson Award, *Food Art*'s Silver Spoon Award, and the James Beard Foundation's Journalism Award and Who's Who of Food & Beverage in America. Her memoir *My Kitchen Wars* was performed in Hollywood and New York as a one-woman show by the actress Dorothy Lyman. Her essay collection, *Eat, Live, Love, Die*, was published in 2016 by Counterpoint Press. She moved back to California to live at Casa Dorinda in Montecito in 2012. Find out more at bettyfussell.com.